TEACH YOUR CHILD TO READ IN
less than
10 MINUTES A DAY!

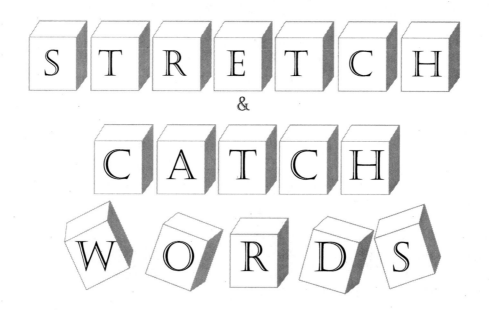

STRETCH

&

CATCH

WORDS

Amanda McNamara Lowe

First published by Dog Ear Publishing
4011 Vincennes Road
Indianapolis, IN 46268
www.dogearpublishing.net

ISBN: 978-1-4575-3809-4

This book is printed on acid free paper.
Printed in the United States of America

To the love of my life, Rick. Thank you for always believing in me.
To my children, Sophia, Thomas, and Addison; thank you for letting me teach you
how to read and spell. You are my muses. To my sisters, Megan and Melissa, for turning my light bulb
on and pushing me forward. To my parents, Walt and Mardy, for all of their love, support, and
guidance. Thank you for being my first editors along with Rick. To Ron for all of his encouragement.
To my in-laws, Dick and Karen, for always being there. To my brother, Walt, I did it.
To my editor, Stephanie, I am so thankful for your fresh set of eyes.
Thank you to all of my friends and family who supported me and believed in me.
I couldn't have written this book without all of the love
and support I received along the way.

TABLE OF CONTENTS

PRE-STRETCH & CATCH

STRETCH & CATCH

THE LAST PHASE OF STRETCH & CATCH

PREFACE

I needed to write this book because teaching children how to read is my passion. I feel that teaching a child to read gives the child all he or she needs to be successful in the world. Once a person can read, his or her ability to learn is limitless. Everyone must read to succeed.

I started my career as a substitute teacher in an ED unit. (ED is the term used for children with emotional disturbances.) I had a bachelor's degree in education and was teaching children with severe special needs. Many of my students had autism, were cognitively challenged, or had learning disabilities on top of being little children with emotional disturbances. Maybe it was my ignorance, as I was only 23, or maybe I just wanted to shine as a new teacher, but I decided that no matter who I was teaching, no matter what disability they had, they would not leave my classroom until they could read.

I was teaching during the day and going to school at night to get my master's degree in moderate to severe special education (to become an intervention specialist). I obtained my master's degree, in 11 months, as well as the designation of intervention specialist. After graduation, I was given the opportunity to continue working in the same special education classroom that I had been working in for the past year, but now I was a genuine special education teacher.

I was determined to teach my students to read. If I didn't teach my students to read, they would be lost, but I knew that if they could learn to read, they would have a chance for success. My students rose to my expectations. With just a few simple steps, all of the students in my room were able to read.

In the midst of teaching my own students to read, I had an opportunity to teach phonics assessment and instruction, as well as literature-based reading programs at Cleveland State University to students getting their undergraduate and graduate degrees in education. I now was going to get to teach adults how to teach children, a dream come true. I taught at Cleveland State University for several years. During my time teaching at Cleveland State, I realized that I loved teaching adults how to teach children to read, as much as, I liked teaching children.

The phonics assessment and instruction I taught to my own students, to my children, and at Cleveland State University used a developmental approach to spelling called Word Study. Word Study was developed by Donald R. Bear, Marcia Invernizzi, Shane Templeton, and Francine Johnston in their book *Words Their Way* (Donald R. Bear, 2000).

I decided to write this book because of my experiences as a teacher, parent, and friend of other parents helping their children read. While I was teaching my own children to read, my friends would tell me how they were trying to help their children but had no idea how or where to start. I thought about that and realized that I could take all the steps I used in my classroom and with my own children to help a lot of parents, caregivers, and teachers teach their own children and students to read. That was when I came up with the Stretch & Catch method.

The Stretch & Catch method combines developmentally appropriate words for Stretch & Catch, high-frequency words that I call The Word List (TWL) words, and daily reading. All together this method creates strong readers. This book therefore incorporates parts of the developmental spelling order developed by Donald R. Bear, Marcia Invernizzi, Shane Templeton, and Francine Johnston in *Words Their Way*, along with my own methods.

It's imperative to stick to the developmental order in this book to successfully teach your child. Throughout this book, the text will read, "your child," but "your student" can be substituted. Many of the activities are geared toward parents, but teachers can also use Stretch & Catch activities within their classroom.

INTRODUCTION

Stretch & Catch words is an easy method that I have developed to help all children learn to read. This book is designed to be an easy guide for parents, caregivers, and teachers who want to teach a child to read. Every child deserves to read, and I truly believe that the Stretch & Catch method of combining developmentally appropriate words for Stretch & Catch, combined with high-frequency words (The Word List words), and daily reading can help all children learn to read.

HOW TO USE THIS BOOK

This section provides an overview of what you will find within each chapter of this book. Please keep in mind that the content covered within this book ranges from preschool to fourth grade. The book is designed to help guide parents with a simple daily activity of 10 minutes or less that will build a strong reading foundation.

The text is designed to be easy to follow. The first chapter explains Stretch & Catch, The Word List (TWL) words, and daily reading. It will explain how and when to teach Stretch & Catch to your child and will also describe the reasoning behind using TWL words and why automaticity is important for every reader. Finally, the chapter will clarify how the daily reading should be completed. At the end of Chapter One are three assessments. The first assessment is on the 26 basic alphabetic sounds. If you are unsure if your child knows his/her basic sounds with a 100% accuracy, you will test him/her using this assessment first. The second assessment is the Feature Assessment Tool. This tool will help the parent know where to start teaching the child at his/her instructional learning level within this book. The last assessment will assess your child on his/her TWL words. The TWL Assessment Tool will help guide you to the correct colored TWL word list for your child.

Chapter Two focuses on the alphabet feature. (When I use the word *feature*, I am referring to the spelling pattern that your child will be learning in the chapter.) This chapter is the Pre-Stretch & Catch chapter and includes daily reading ideas for the parent. Before your child can Stretch & Catch, he/she will need to be able to identify the 26 basic alphabetic sounds. Beginning with Chapter Three, you will introduce your child to the Stretch & Catch features and TWL words, and the daily reading will continue. Chapter Three focuses on Features 2–6 from the assessment, which are short-vowel words.

Chapter Four covers Features 7–11. Here, your child will begin to blend two letters together at the beginnings and endings of words. These words are referred to as beginning and ending blends.

Chapter Five, with Features 12 and 13, introduces digraphs. This is the first chapter in which your child will learn that the number of sounds heard in a word won't always correspond with the number of letters that are actually in that word.

Chapters Six through Nine, covering Features 14–26, enter the last phase of Stretch & Catch. This is referred to as the last phase because it is the phase which your child moves from a beginning reader to a more advanced independent reader. Beginning with these chapters, you will notice that your child will lead the Stretch & Catch activity while you will be there to guide your child. TWL words will continue to be present in Chapters Six and Seven but won't be needed by Chapters Eight and Nine because your child now has a stronger word and spelling foundation and will be able to figure out unknown words by using the Stretch & Catch Reading Strategy and context clues. In all of these chapters, the daily reading is extremely important for your child's reading success. By the end of this book, your child will transition from reading aloud to a silent reader.

Starting with Chapter Five and moving through Chapter Nine, an optional activity is included to introduce each feature before you Stretch & Catch. Although this is an optional activity, it would be very beneficial for your child. If you do not have time for this activity, that is okay; the Stretch & Catch templates will help provide the introduction to the features as well.

A WORD ABOUT NOTE CARDS

For the lessons in this book, I suggest purchasing a 500 pack of 3x5 white note cards. The note cards will be used to reinforce the lesson in Chapter Two for the alphabet. In Chapters Three- Nine, there will also be optional activities to reinforce the feature you will be teaching by using the note cards. You will also write The Word List (TWL) words on the note cards.

For Chapter Two, you will need 52 note cards. Make one note card per letter for each uppercase letter and one note card per letter for each lowercase letter. Consonants should be written in one color, while vowels should be written in a different color. It is important that the consonants are written in a different color than the vowel note cards because you want to make a distinction between consonants and vowels in this chapter.

In Chapters Five through Nine, there are optional activities to reinforce the spelling pattern your child learned by using note cards. If you chose to use either of the optional activities that appear before or after the features, you will need to prepare the note cards before you teach the lesson.

You can continue to use the lowercase note cards from Chapter Two throughout this book, but you will also need to make additional consonant and vowel note cards because there will be words with duplicate letters. Once your child understand the difference between consonants and vowels, all the letter note cards can be written in the same color.

You will also need to write TWL words in the corresponding colors (blue, orange, green, red, and purple) for Chapters Three through Seven on your note cards.

CHAPTER ONE

PREPARATION AND ASSESSMENT

WHAT IS STRETCH & CATCH?

In order to learn how to read, a child must understand how words work. By learning how to Stretch & Catch words, your child will use many of his/her senses to see how words are put together and pulled apart. This combined with The Word List (TWL) words (a list of high-frequency words that can make up 50% or more of a reading text) and daily reading will create a reader in your child.

The idea behind Stretch & Catch is for children to learn how to see patterns within words and then sound out words by using their ears to hear the sounds, their mouths to feel sounds, and their fingers to see sounds.

The more a child is exposed throughout the day to letters, sounds, and words, the faster those letters, sounds, and words will begin to imprint (be memorized) in the child's brain. Any time you have five minutes, you have time to Stretch & Catch.

Stretch & Catch follows a technique that allows the adult to teach a child how to spell while using their fingers to Stretch (sound out the word by raising one finger at a time per sound) and then Catch the word by saying all the sounds quickly while bringing the fingers into a fist. You will find that Catching the word is not an important piece of spelling words, but as your child grows into a reader and is Stretching or sounding out unknown words in text, he/she will then need to Catch those sounds to read the word. I therefore include Stretching & Catching together throughout this book so it becomes automatic to your child when he/she needs that skill in reading.

Below, you will find an example of a beginning lesson in Chapter Three, "Short Vowels," with an adult Stretching & Catching the short-vowel word **dot**. This example is from Feature 5 lesson 3 (5-3).

[Note that if I want you to say a sound and not a letter, the sound will be placed between two slanted lines and in bold print. For example, when I want you to say the short-**a** sound, it will look like this: /**ă**/. When I want you to say the name of the letter **A**, it will be capitalized and in bold print.]

Stretch & Catch short-vowel word: **dot**

Step 1: Say, "We are going to spell the word **dot**." Now tell your child: "When I say /**d**/ [sound the letter out and lift the first finger], /**ŏ**/ [sound the letter out and lift the second finger], /**t**/ [sound the letter out and lift the third finger], do you see that I hear three sounds? So if I hear three sounds, there are three letters. Let's see what three letters we hear." Leave your fingers up.

Step 2: Say the following: "When I say **dot**, I hear /**d**/ [wriggle or point to your first finger]. What letter is the /**d**/ sound?" If your child says the letter **D**, that is great. If your child gives an incorrect response, model that the **D** sound is /**d**/, like in **dog** (dog is the key word for the **D** sound). *You will be given a list of key words in Chapter Two to use for each letter sound. This will be used to model the correct response.*

Step 3: Your fingers are still up. Sound out the word again, stopping at the second sound. "/**d**/ [wriggle/point to first finger], /**ŏ**/ [wriggle/point to second finger]." Continue to say, "I hear the vowel sound /**ŏ**/. [Wriggle/point to the second finger.] What letter makes the /**ŏ**/ sound?" If your child gives the correct response, great. If not, model the correct response: "The /**ŏ**/ sound is the letter **O**, as in **octopus**." *Again, notice the use of the key word to model the correct response.*

Step 4: Move on to the last sound. Sound out the word again. (Your fingers are still up.) "/**d**/ [wriggle/point to first finger], /**ŏ**/ [wriggle/point to second finger], /**t**/ [wriggle/point to third finger]." Emphasize the last sound while pointing to or wriggling the third finger again. "What is the last sound you hear in **dot**?" Make sure to emphasize the /**t**/ sound. If your child gets the answer correct, great; if not, model the correct response: "When I hear the word **dot,** I hear the /**t**/ sound at the end. The /**t**/sound is a **T**, like in **top** [keyword]." Now put the three fingers down.

Step 5: *Stretch* the word again: "/**d**/ [sound the letter out and lift the first finger], /**ŏ**/ [sound the letter out and lift the second finger], /**t**/ [sound the letter out and lift the third finger]."

Step 6: "**Dot** is spelled **D** [wriggle/point to first finger], **O** [wriggle/point to second finger], **T** [wriggle/point to third finger]."

Step 7: Then Catch the word by saying it fast and pulling the three fingers into a fist: "**Dot.**"

You catch the word because your child needs to practice pulling apart and putting words back together so he/she can hear each word he/she Stretches. This technique will be crucial when your child sees an unknown word while reading and begins to Stretch it out. For him/her to figure out the unknown word, he/she will have to Catch it after Stretching it by saying it quickly to identify what word he/she Stretched.

Step 8: Now say, "Did you see how I did that? That's how you Stretch & Catch words."

Optional: Finally, use the note cards to show your child the letters that make up the word and have him/her manipulate the cards to make the new word.

Optional: Ask your child to identify the consonants and vowel in each word.

Optional: Use word cards to practice the Stretch & Catch Reading Strategy.

After your child completes each Stretch & Catch exercise, you will have a chance to reinforce each word by using note cards to remake the word. You will need to use your lowercase letter cards that you made in Chapter Two to make the words, or you can make new lowercase letter cards for each exercise. When you Stretch & Catch a word, you will want to have a note card for each letter in that word. This is helpful so the child can actually see the letters and manipulate the letters to make a word. This will help him/her practice Stretch & Catch in reading, because the more your child plays with words, the faster his/her brain will understand pulling apart words and putting words together, which is an important skill your child needs for reading. This will also reinforce the word in your child's brain. The more your child can actually spell, see, and make words; the higher the chance the word will become imprinted into his/her brain. Once a word is imprinted into a child's brain, it becomes automatic so the child can identify the word without sounding it out every time. Adults do this automatically while reading. You will find the Stretch & Catch Reading Strategy explanation later in this chapter.

In the beginning of Stretch & Catch, your child will first learn how to spell words by seeing your fingers Stretch & Catch the word. As your child moves through the lessons, he/she will begin to Stretch & Catch using his/her own fingers. Then as your child begins to read early readers (easy books designed for beginning readers), you will help him/her use his/her own fingers to Stretch & Catch appropriate words within each book. (This is referred to as Stretch & Catch Reading Strategy and will be explained later in this chapter.) As your child practices and develops all of these skills while having a greater background of instruction in spelling, he/she will be able to look at a word within a text, find the spelling pattern of the unknown word, and then Stretch & Catch the unknown word within his/her head.

What is unique about this program is that it follows a developmental order of spelling; it coordinates your child's fingers to each sound so your child can see, touch, and hear the letters in the word, while also combining the high-frequency words in TWL and daily reading. A combination of all of these methods together makes the Stretch & Catch method a successful program.

WHAT ARE TWL WORDS?

In addition to Stretch & Catch features, your child will be given five colored lists of high-frequency words that he/she must be able to identify automatically without sounding out. In this book, I have provided my own list of high-frequency words and words that cannot be sounded out. I call these The Word List (TWL) words. In the beginning chapters, TWL words are extremely important because they tend to be irregular and are not able to be sounded out or because they appear so frequently in text that your child should know the word automatically. These TWL words can make up 50%–60% of your child's reading. If your child is fluent and automatic with TWL, he/she will be less frustrated while learning to read.

These words need to be automatic when your child reads them. A TWL list is placed at the beginning of Chapter Three, Four, Five, Six, and Seven. The TWL list does not correspond to the feature that your child will be learning in each chapter.

I tried to make the beginning TWL words a little easier for a beginning reader. To help, I also provided some words within groups. For example, in the red TWL words, your child will encounter color and number words; some of these words will be easy for your child to sound out, but the idea is that these words are used so frequently in books that your child must know them automatically, without sounding them out.

Being fluent and automatic with TWL words provides less frustration to your child while he/she is learning to read; therefore, if your child has memorized TWL for each chapter, he/she will be able to identify those specific words with no frustration while reading.

Your child can't move to the next TWL until he/she has mastered the list with 100% accuracy. The TWL words don't correspond with each Stretch & Catch chapter, so if your child moves quickly through the TWL words but not quickly through the Stretch & Catch chapters, you may move on to the next TWL words. You may also move to the next Stretch & Catch chapter if your child has mastered all of the features within that chapter but has not mastered TWL within that chapter. Think of each color-coded TWL as a separate set of features. Your child can move forward in this set of features while staying in place in the Stretch & Catch features, and vice versa.

HOW DO I KNOW MY CHILD IS READY TO STRETCH & CATCH?

To Stretch & Catch words, your child must be able to dictate the 26 letters of the alphabet, be able to identify all 26 printed lowercase and uppercase letters, and be able to identify all 26 basic alphabetic sounds. (For vowels, this means the short vowel sounds that represent the vowels.) If your child does not know the 26 basic alphabetic sounds, you will begin in Chapter Two, which consists only of teaching the 26 basic alphabetic sounds to your child.

You will begin by assessing your child on the 26 basic alphabetic sounds. You will find the assessment page with a list of the 26 basic alphabetic sounds at the end of this chapter.

HOW TO START STRETCH & CATCH?

You will start Stretch & Catch first by using the assessment tool at the end of this chapter. This tool will help guide you in deciding which chapter to begin with. After you assess your child and choose the correct chapter, you can begin to Stretch & Catch with him/her. Each chapter will be different. Some chapters might have features that your child excels in and that he/she finishes the features quickly. Other chapters have very difficult features that may take your child several months to a year to master. This book is designed to fit within your child's ability level and pace. There is no time limit on any chapter. The features within this book span from preschool to fourth grade. Use this book as a tool. Please do not feel that your child needs to quickly pass through each feature. This book will be your guide for years with your child. It is designed to help guide you with developmentally appropriate words using a method that will help your child conquer reading. It is important that you don't move ahead until your child has mastered each feature. At the end of each feature, you will know if your child can move on by giving him/her an assessment from the assessment tool provided within this chapter.

There are three levels of learning: independent, instructional, and frustrated. The independent level is where your child can easily read words and needs no instructional help. The frustrated level is where your child is so overwhelmed that he/she gets angry, starts to cry, and feels overwhelmed by any of the words. He/she is frustrated even with guidance. Teach your child only at his instructional level. This is the level at which your child finds the words too hard at first but, with your instruction, begins to learn the words in a non-stressful environment. This is the level that all children should be taught at. This is the level in which they will learn how to read. If your child becomes frustrated at any time, try to slow down. Some children will only want to Stretch & Catch one or two words per day. Allow your child to move at his/her own pace.

Remember, you will decide which lesson your child should begin with by giving him/her the assessment. This assessment is given only to children who have mastered the 26 basic alphabetic sounds. If your child has mastered the alphabetic sounds but has never learned how to spell words, you will not need to assess your child and will begin automatically with Chapter Three. The assessment is given initially only if you are unsure as to which chapter/feature to begin with.

You will begin by going to the assessment page. The assessment page will be divided into two categories: features and TWL words. The features and TWL words do not go hand in hand and therefore have separate assessments. You will know where to start in the book by first assessing your child on the features. Once your child has received a 70% or below on a feature, you will stop assessing him/her and begin with that feature within this book.

Next, you will assess your child on his/her TWL words. TWL words are assigned to each chapter, but once your child has mastered one set of TWL words with 100% accuracy, he/she will move on to the next TWL words, regardless of which feature he/she is on. Your child must have 100% accuracy on TWL words and Feature 1 (26 basic alphabetic sounds) before moving on, whereas he/she needs only 80% accuracy for Features 2–26 to move on. If your child receives an 80% on a feature and you don't feel he/she has mastered that feature, you can still teach that feature to your child. The assessment tool is only a guide; you as the parent can ultimately decide where to place your child within this book.

HOW TO TEACH TWL WORDS

Each set of TWL words that your child must memorize is color-coded. It is important that you keep the color coding so your child can see his/her progress within each TWL list. You can print a copy of the colored word list from my website (using a color printer), or you may write the words using the designated color on a white note card.

Each week, you will introduce TWL words from the list for your child. Every child learns at a different rate, and some children can handle learning many words at one time, while other children get frustrated with more than one word per day. Once you get to know your child's capabilities, you will know how many words to introduce. Therefore, start with 5 TWL words per week. The key is to compile the words into categories of "known words" and "need-more-practice words." Introduce one word each day of the week. If your child automatically recognizes the word, then it is a "known" word. If your child is struggling on the word or trying to sound the word out, you will assist him/her by telling him/her the word and placing it in the "need-more-practice" category. If your child is able to quickly master 5 TWL words, you may continue adding words for that week. You will introduce only the number of words that your child is capable of mastering in one week's time.

It is important to display each "known" word somewhere in your house where your child can see it. This not only lets the child see what he/she has accomplished but also allows you to quickly review your child's "known" words with him/her. I suggest reviewing the "known" words each day before introducing the new word. Some examples of places to hang your child's TWL words might include a bulletin board in his/her room, his/her bedroom door, the refrigerator, or around a doorframe.

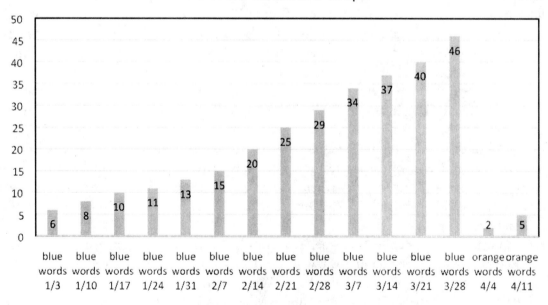

The Word List Word Graph

Another way to track your child's progress is by making a bar graph of your child's weekly "known" TWL words. The graph shown here represents the progress of a child who progressed through the blue TWL words. This child began with only six "known" words the first week and then progressively increased the "known" blue words for three months until mastery. This graph represents an example of progressing through one TWL word list and moving on to the next TWL word list. Notice how this child moved on to the orange words once the blue words were mastered.

DAILY READING

Daily reading is an important piece of teaching your child how to read. In Chapter Two, your child will be learning the alphabet and basic alphabetic sounds. During this time, it is important to read many alphabet books with your child. The more you expose your child to the alphabet and the alphabetic sounds, the faster his/her brain will memorize them.

In Chapters Three through Six, your child will be introduced to TWL words, as well as begin to Stretch & Catch short-vowel words, beginning and ending blends, and digraphs. It is important to read early reader books with your child while he/she is learning these features. Your local librarian can help you pick out books that are designed for early readers; such books include limited vocabulary, short-vowel words, predictable patterns, picture clues, and many high-frequency words. At first, you will need to be the primary reader for your child. As your child memorizes more TWL words and begins to master the features, he/she will be able to take over part of the reading. When you come across a word that contains a Stretch & Catch feature that your child has mastered or is working on, stop and allow him/her to Stretch & Catch the word. If at any time you come to a TWL word that your child has mastered or has been introduced to, stop and see if your child can identify the TWL word.

As you move through the features and TWL words, you will notice that your child is becoming a reader. When your child can easily read early readers to you without assistance, it is time to move to leveled reading books. Many different series have levels, steps, or ages assigned to each book. These guidelines can help a parent pick the "just right" book for his/her child. You will know your child is ready to move to the next step or level book when he/she is able to easily read a book without any assistance.

In Chapter Six, you will notice that your child is becoming a more fluent reader. You can still use leveled or step books during this time, but your child can also explore a variety of children's books that interest him/her. It is important to know your child's interests so you can pick the right books for him/her. Some children love reading fiction books. Other children love reading nonfiction books. Nonfiction books are great because your child can learn about subjects he/she is passionate about. No matter what books your child loves, you can find some at your local library to pique his/her interest. Whether your child loves to read fiction or nonfiction books, it is important is that he/she reads each day.

While your child is reading aloud to you, make sure he/she is paying attention to punctuation. You also want to encourage him/her to use expression while reading.

As your child progresses through Chapters Seven, Eight, and Nine, he/she is not only fluent while reading but also has expression while reading. With your child's deep understanding of spelling, combined with the vast amount of TWL words memorized, your child will transition in these chapters from reading aloud to being a silent reader.

HOW DO I USE STRETCH & CATCH AS A READING STRATEGY?

The idea behind Stretch & Catch Reading Strategy is to begin to teach your child the Stretch & Catch strategy to figuring out unknown words while reading. This will be an optional activity that you can do daily with your child. Simply use the examples below to work on the Stretch & Catch Reading Strategy with each feature your child is working in. It's a simple idea.

- First, your child looks at the unknown word within a book. Then, your child will look at the unknown word for a pattern. (The pattern is also referred to as the feature; they are interchangeable.) Having your child look for patterns within each word begins to train your child's brain to look at an entire word before sounding it out or guessing while reading. (People who have mastered reading automatically find the patterns within unknown words while reading.)

- Second, the child Stretches the word while putting up his/her own finger for each sound in the unknown word. If this is too difficult for your child, you can lift a finger per each sound your child sounds out. This allows the child to see and hear the sounds within a word. If it is too hard for your child at first to even Stretch [sound out] the word, you may model the Stretch & Catch Reading Strategy any time you get to a word in a book in which your child has learned that feature. The more your child watches you model, the sooner he/she will be able to use the Stretch & Catch Reading Strategy without assistance.

- Last, the child Catches the word. This allows the child to quickly pull the sounds back together to figure out the unknown word. Again, if this is too hard for your child at first, model for him/her how to Catch a word after you have Stretched it out.

You can practice the Stretch & Catch Reading Strategy daily within the feature your child is working on or has worked on. Simply write the feature words on a card and have your child Stretch & Catch the unknown word on each card. You can add this to your daily Stretch & Catch routine. If you do not have time to use the Stretch & Catch Reading Strategy using the feature words on note cards, you can have your child practice any time he/she comes to an unknown word within a book that contains a feature he/she has learned.

The following examples use both methods to practice the Stretch & Catch Reading Strategy. The first example uses the note cards of the words within the feature your child is working on. The second example is of a child reading a book and using the Stretch & Catch Reading Strategy to figure out an unknown word.

EXAMPLE EXERCISE USING NOTE CARDS

This example is from Chapter Three, Feature 2, Lesson 1 (2-1): **short ă: at words**
Feature word note card: **sat**

Step 1: Adult: "What is the pattern within this word?" [You want your child to identify that the pattern is a short-**a** (ă) word.] Move to Step 2 if your child is able to identify the pattern. If your child is unable to identify the pattern of this word, move to the bullet point below.

- Adult: "When I see the letter **A** in the middle of a word, I know it makes that word have an /ă/ sound like in **apple**." Move to the next step.

Step 2: Adult: "Let's Stretch & Catch this word." If your child is unable to Stretch this word, move to the bullet points below. Otherwise, move to the next step.

- The adult will say, "/**s**/ [adult's first finger up], /**ă**/ [adult's second finger up], /**t**/ [adult's third finger up]."
- Now the adult will catch the word. "**Sat.**" Catch the word by saying it quickly and bringing all three fingers back into a fist. Move to Step 3.

Step 3: Have your child Stretch the word out: "/**s**/ [child's first finger up], /**ă**/ [child's second finger up], /**t**/ [child's third finger up]."

Step 4: Have your child Catch the word: "**Sat.**" (Have your child Catch the word by saying it quickly and bringing all three of his/her fingers back into a fist.)

EXAMPLE EXERCISE USING AN UNKNOWN WORD IN A BOOK

This example is from Chapter Five, Feature 12, Lesson 4 (12-4): **beginning digraphs.**
Unknown word in book: **champ**

Step 1: Child: "I see this word that I don't know."

Step 2: Adult: "Let's Stretch & Catch it to find out what the word is."

Step 3: Adult: "First, you need to look at the word. Do you see a pattern in this word?"

Step 4: You want to encourage your child to recognize the features within the word. In the example word **champ**, the features you want your child to be aware of are: beginning digraph (**CH**), a short-a (ă) vowel, and a special ending blend (**MP**). If your child is aware of these features, he/she will know that this word has more letters than sounds, move to Step 5. If your child does not see the features, move to the bullet point below.

- Say: "This word has a digraph at the beginning of the word, so even though we see five letters, we will use only four sounds to sound it out. This word also contains a short-a (ă) sound and has a blend of **MP** at the end of the word." Move to Step 5.

Step 5: Adult: "Let's Stretch & Catch this word." If your child is unable to Stretch this word, move to the bullet points below. Otherwise, move to Step 6.

- Say, "/**ch**/ [adult's first finger up], /ă/ [adult's second finger up], /**m**/ [adult's third finger up], /**p**/ [adult's fourth finger up]."
- Now the adult will catch the word. "**Champ.**" Catch the word by saying it quickly and bringing all fingers back into a fist. Move to Step 6 so your child can Stretch & Catch the word.

Step 6: Have your child Stretch the word: "/**ch**/ [child's first finger up], /ă/ [child's second finger up], /**m**/ [child's third finger up], /**p**/ [child's fourth finger up]."

Step 7: Have your child Catch the word: "**Champ.**"

HOW DO I PICK A "JUST RIGHT" BOOK FOR MY CHILD?

As your child progresses through the features, he/she will begin to read more books on his/her own, but how will you or your child know if a book is "just right" for him/her?

You will use the five-finger test. Open the book and have your child read a page (at least 5 sentences). Tell your child to start with all of his/her fingers down. For every word your child is unable to pronounce, have your child put one finger up.

- Zero fingers: Easy (independent level)
- One finger: Easy
- Two fingers: Just right
- Three fingers: A little challenging (instructional level)
- Four fingers: Can try but might be very challenging
- Five fingers: Too hard (frustration level)

Independent Level *(0–2 fingers):* At this level, your child will feel very comfortable reading a book on his/her own. Your child can use these types of books to practice his/her fluency while reading. This is also a good level to practice expression and review punctuation while reading (quotation marks, commas, periods).

Instructional Level *(3–4 fingers):* At this level, your child can try to read the book independently, but it might be too challenging. This is a good book for your child to read aloud to you so you will be there to guide him/her through words that he/she is unable to pronounce, sound out, or understand.

Frustration Level *(5 fingers):* This book would be too challenging for your child to read on his/her own but can be read by an adult. Children can understand a story that is above their instructional level when it is read to them.

HOW TO PREPARE FOR EACH LESSON

Before each lesson, make sure to have the list of words that your child will be Stretching & Catching. In addition to the regular Stretching & Catching activities, there are two optional activities at the end of every Stretch & Catch. The first optional activity is for your child to use lowercase letter note cards to make the word that he/she just spelled. If you choose to have your child participate in this activity, you will need to make the letter note cards for every word your child Stretches & Catches within that feature. For example, if your child just finished Stretching & Catching the word **that**, you will need four letter note cards (**t, h, a, t**).

The second optional activity is to have your child practice the Stretch & Catch Reading Strategy. In order for your child to participate in this activity, you will need to write the words from the feature on each note card. Then you will have your child use the Stretch & Catch Reading Strategy to read the note cards.

In Chapters Five through Nine, there will be an optional activity to introduce each feature before you Stretch & Catch. Although this is an optional activity, it would be very beneficial to use this activity when you introduce each new feature. If you do not have time for this activity, that is okay, because the Stretch & Catch templates will provide bullet points within the activity that will help explain and guide your child through the feature he/she is struggling with. If you do have time for this activity, you will need to make the note cards with the words from the lesson/feature (one on each note card) you are introducing.

These additional activities are provided for you only if you have time. If your child is struggling with any feature, it is a good idea to have him/her complete the additional activities to reinforce the feature.

FEATURE ASSESSMENT TOOL

To identify which feature your child will begin with, you will need to assess your child using the feature assessment tool below. A feature is a spelling pattern. You will begin with Feature 1: identifies all 26 basic sounds of the alphabet. If your child is able to identify with 100% accuracy all of the basic 26 sounds of the alphabet, move on to the Feature 2 assessment. The Feature 1 assessment requires 100% accuracy to move on to Feature 2, but Features 2–26 require your child to have only an 80% accuracy to move to the next feature.

If you are unsure which feature your child's instruction should begin with, start your assessment on Feature 1. The tool you will use to help you assess your child's accuracy within this feature can be found at the beginning of the assessment tools. Each letter is in the chart. Simply point to the letter and ask your child to say the sound of that letter. If your child identifies the sound correctly, place a check in the column next to that letter. If your child is unable to identify the sound, place an X on the chart. You will notice that there are several columns next to each letter. Each column will represent a different date that you assessed your child. If your child identifies all 26 sounds correctly the first time the assessment is given, there will be no use for the extra columns. Once your child has completed Feature 1 with 100% accuracy, you will move on to Feature 2.

If your child can already identify the 26 basic sounds of the alphabet and you don't know where to begin instruction, you will begin by assessing your child in Feature 2. You will assess your child by having him/her spell the words in the Feature 2 chart. Circle any word your child misses out of the 10 words that are given. If your child spells 8–10 of the words correctly, you will mark his/her score in the column marked "Mastered Score/Date" and move to the next feature. Continue to assess your child and mark his/her score in the "Mastered Score/Date" if he/she has a score of 8–10. A score of 8–10 is your child's independent level of spelling, and your child will not need to be instructed on this feature.

The first feature in which your child spells 7 or fewer words correctly is the feature where you will begin your instruction. Mark the column with your child's score and date. The date is important so you can track your child's progress throughout the book. At any time during a lesson that you feel your child has mastered the feature, you may give him/her this quick assessment to see if he/she is ready to move on to the next feature.

This assessment is only a tool to help you, the parent, know where to start your child in Stretch & Catch and when to move on. If you feel your child is able to move on to the next feature without an 80% accuracy rate on the feature assessment, then do so. I want this assessment to be a useful tool, but it is not the only tool to measure your child's ability. It is simply here to help guide you through the Stretch & Catch features.

26 BASIC ALPHABETIC SOUND ASSESSMENT TOOL

26 Basic Sounds of the Alphabet	Date Assessed	Date Assessed	Date Assessed	Date Assessed	Date Assessed	Date Assessed	Date Assessed
a							
b							
c							
d							
e							
f							
g							
h							
i							
j							
k							
l							
m							
n							
o							
p							
q							
r							
s							
t							
u							
v							
w							
x							
y							
z							

FEATURE ASSESSMENT TOOL

Chapter/ Feature	Feature	Score/ Date	Score/ Date	Score/ Date	Mastered Score/ Date
Chapter 2 Feature 1	**Identifies all 26 basic sounds of the alphabet.**				
Chapter 3 Feature 2	ă: cat, hat, bag, rag, can, pan, cap, lap, sad, ham				
Chapter 3 Feature 3	ĕ: bet, let, set, met, led, bed, fed, beg, leg, peg				
Chapter 3 Feature 4	ĭ: bit, kit, did, hid, big, dig, bin, pin, dim, him				
Chapter 3 Feature 5	ŏ: cop, pop, mop, dog, fog, cot, got, cob, rob, job				
Chapter 3 Feature 6	ŭ: rut, nut, cub, rub, bug, sub, gum, sum, bun, fun				
Chapter 4 Feature 7	**S Blends**: stop, stem, spit, spat, slip, snot, snip, skim, skip, swam				
Chapter 4 Feature 8	**L Blends**: blip, blot, glam, glad, flag, flop, clam, clip, plug, plus				
Chapter 4 Feature 9	**R Blends**: trip, trim, drip, drop, brad, brag, frog, fret, Fred, trot				
Chapter 4 Feature 10	**Ending Blends**: mask, task, just, must, lost, best, raft, left, shelf, self				

Chapter 4 Feature 11	**Special Ending Blends:** lamp, jump, hand, band, mint, stint, skunk, drink, stink, blink				
Chapter 5 Feature 12	**Digraphs:** ship, shop, this, them, thin, think, whim, whip, chant, champ				
Chapter 5 Feature 13	**Ending Digraphs:** flash, crash, rich, much, bath, math, stuck, check duck, stick				
Chapter 6 Feature 14	**āCe:** lake, plate, face, whale, grape, lane, tape, cane, mate, plane				
Chapter 6 Feature 15	**īCe:** dice, lime, mile, mine, wipe, kite, pine, spite, ripe, time				
Chapter 6 Feature 16	**ōCe:** bone, choke, stone, wrote, drove, note, tone, hope, code, robe				
Chapter 6 Feature 17	**ūCe:** muse, rude, dude, brute, dune, plume, cute, use, huge, cube				
Chapter 7 Feature 18	**Other Common ā Patterns:** main, aid, pain, paid, jail, may, slay, way, play, pay				
Chapter 7 Feature 19	**Other Common ē Patterns:** sweep, breed, greet, cream, reach, beach, scream, me, she, be				

Chapter 7 Feature 20	**Other Common ī Patterns:** shy, bye, rye, might, tight, flight, fright, find, kind, blind				
Chapter 7 Feature 21	**Other Common ō Patterns:** hold, bold, told, roast, boast, groan, foam, throw, grow, know				
Chapter 7 Feature 22	**Other Common ū Patterns:** clue, blue, fruit, cruise, juice, flew, knew, stew, room, moon				
Chapter 8 Feature 23	**Diphthongs:** enjoy, soy, avoid, oil, voice, shout, count, mound, clown, brown				
Chapter 9 Feature 24	**R-Controlled Patterns with /ar/ vs /air/ sound:** dark, far, part, care, scare, share, dare, pair, stair, flair				
Chapter 9 Feature 25	**R-Controlled Patterns with /ear/ sound:** near, clear, dear, fear, year, cheer, sheer, peer, deer, beer				
Chapter 9 Feature 26	**R-Controlled Patterns /or/ vs /er/ sound:** stern, perch, surf, hurt, burn, thirsty, thirty, chirp, short, sport				

*You will notice that in chapter six there is no feature for long ēCe [long /ē/ words]. There are very few words that follow this patterns so it will not be taught in this book. Your child will learn long ē sounds in chapter seven.

TWL ASSESSMENT TOOL

The words for each assessment are located at the beginning of each chapter. Have your child read each word to you. Mark the number correct & the date in each column. A score of 100% is required before moving on to the next TWL Assessment.

BLUE TWL Word Assessment

Chapter Three

Number Correct of 46	Date Assessed

ORANGE TWL Word Assessment

Chapter Four

Number Correct of 40	Date Assessed

GREEN TWL Word Assessment

Chapter Five

Number Correct of 65	Date Assessed

RED TWL Word Assessment

Chapter Six

Number Correct of 54	Date Assessed

PURPLE TWL Word Assessment

Chapter Seven

Number Correct of 61	Date Assessed

PRE-STRETCH & CATCH

CHAPTER TWO

THE 26 BASIC ALPHABETIC SOUNDS

DAILY READING

For your child to begin to understand how letters make words and words together make stories, you will need to read to your child daily. Exposing children to many books helps them become beginning readers. While you read, your child observes how books open, how you read from left to right, and how the pictures in the book and the words work together to form a story. These are all important beginning reader skills. When you come to a word with a beginning sound that you have already taught your child, simply say the word and ask him/her if he/she knows the beginning sound. You want your child to begin to understand that the stories you read are made up of letters, those letters form words, and those words form stories.

THE 26 BASIC ALPHABETIC SOUNDS

The goal of this chapter is to teach your child the 26 alphabetic sounds. It is imperative that your child understand that the letters in the alphabet make sounds. As your child moves through the different features, he/she will be exposed to the many sounds that letters can make. In this feature, your child will be learning only the 26 basic letter sounds, which include the short vowel sounds for **A, E, I, O,** and **U.** By the end of this feature, your child needs to be able to identify all 26 letter sounds. You will know when your child is ready to move on to the next feature by giving him/her the 26 Basic Alphabetic Sound Assessment Tool from Chapter One.

This chapter provides a daily activity to do with your child. This activity will take a few minutes, and then you will need to reinforce the alphabet sounds throughout the day.

HOW DO I TEACH THE 26 BASIC ALPHABETIC SOUNDS?

1. Have your alphabet note cards prepared. Make one note card for each uppercase letter and one note card for each lowercase letter. Consonants should be written in one color, and vowels should be written in a different color. It is important that the consonants and vowels are different colors because you want to make a distinction between consonants and vowels in this chapter.
2. Introduce one letter/sound per day. If this is the very first time your child is being exposed to the alphabet sounds, you will introduce one letter/sound per week. Simply replace "day" with "week" throughout this feature.
3. Discuss only short vowels when referring to the vowels (**A, E, I, O, U**).
    When I refer to sound within this book, the sound will be placed between two slanted lines and in bold print. For example, when I want you to say the short-a sound, it will look like this: /ă/. When I want you to say the name of the letter A, it will be capitalized and in bold print.

    a. I will mark the short vowels with a breve mark above the vowel (while the long vowel will have a macron, which will be discussed in later chapters.) The breve mark helps you know it's a short vowel sound. The short vowels will be marked like this: /ă/, /ĕ/, / ĭ/, /ŏ/, /ŭ/. A short vowel makes only one sound. The **A** says **apple**, E says **egg**, the **I** says **itch**, the **O** says **octopus**, and the **U** says **up**. If the vowel says any other sound, it is not a short vowel. These five words will be your vowel **key words**. Key words are used to remind your child of a sound. For example: "Remember the letter **A** says **apple**."

b. If your child is having a hard time grasping the alphabetic sounds, don't worry. The few minutes of daily repetition will help your child learn all the letter sounds. Each child learns at a different rate, so don't get frustrated if mastering the alphabetic sounds is difficult for your child at first. You may at any time introduce a letter a week instead of a letter a day if that is better for your child.

4. Each time you review, make sure you show your child the upper- and lowercase letter that goes with each sound you are reviewing. You want your child to use as many senses as possible to learn the alphabet. With the note cards, he/she will be able to touch the letter cards, see the letter cards, hear the sounds when you say them, hear the sounds when he/she says them, then finally feel the sounds in his/her mouth when he/she says them. The more senses used and the more your child is exposed to the alphabet sounds, the faster your child will grasp each sound.

Each letter will have one **key word** that is in bold print. This key word is the one word you want your child to think of every time he/she hears the sound that word is affiliated with. For example, the /ă/ sound will always be affiliated with the word **apple**. Therefore, every time your child forgets what the /ă/ sound is, you will remind him/her with this statement: "Remember, the **A** says **apple**."

KEY WORDS

A: apple	**N: no**
B: baby	**O: octopus**
C: cat	**P: popsicle**
D: dog	**Q: queen**
E: egg	**R: run**
F: fish	**S: so**
G: go	**T: top**
H: house	**U: up**
I: itch	**V: van**
J: jump	**W: we**
K: kite	**X: box**
L: lollipop	**Y: yes**
M: mom	**Z: zip**

A LETTER A DAY

(5–10 minutes)

LETTER A

<u>BEFORE THE LESSON</u>: Start by introducing the upper- and lowercase letter cards, saying, "This is the letter **A**. See how the letter is big and little? The big letter is called the uppercase letter, and the little letter is called the lowercase letter. They are both the same letter, and they both have the same sound."

<u>AFTER THE LESSON</u>: At any time during the day, you can reinforce the letters you have taught. For example, you can say to your child, "I see an apple. Apple. What letter does *apple* begin with?" (Make sure to emphasize the first letter when teaching beginning sounds.)

A *followed by R, L, or W doesn't make the short-A (ă) sound (though there are always exceptions to this rule). You don't need to point this out to your child now, but you, as the parent, need to know that* car, ball, *and* raw *don't make the /ă/ sound.*

A

The **A** says /ă/, as in **apple**, ant, act.
The letter **A** is called a vowel.
Now we are going to think of words that begin with the letter **A**.
Can you think of any other words that begin with the /ă/ sound?

Here are some /ă/ words to help you along: after, animal, and, ask, at, an, ax, ant, actor.

apple

LETTER B

<u>BEFORE THE LESSON</u>: Start by introducing the upper- and lowercase letter cards, saying, "This is the letter **B**. See how the letter is big and little? The big letter is called the uppercase letter, and the little letter is called the lowercase letter. They are both the same letter, and they both have the same sound."

<u>AFTER THE LESSON</u>: At any time during the day, you can reinforce the letters you have taught. For example, you can say to your child, "I see a boy. Boy. What letter does *boy* begin with?" (Make sure to emphasize the first letter when teaching beginning sounds.)

Let's review:

The **A** says /ă/, as in **apple**, ant, act.

B

Now we are going to learn the letter **B** sound.
The letter **B** is called a consonant.
The **B** says **baby**, big, box.
Can you think of any other words that begin with the letter **B**?

baby

Here are some B words to help you along: boy, bed, ball, big, box, bell, bus, bike, boat, bird, book, blanket, beach, bee, bag.

LETTER C

<u>BEFORE THE LESSON</u>: Start by introducing the upper- and lowercase letter cards, saying, "This is the letter **C**. See how the letter is big and little? The big letter is called the uppercase letter, and the little letter is called the lowercase letter. They are both the same letter, and they both have the same sound."

<u>AFTER THE LESSON</u>: At any time during the day, you can reinforce the letters you have taught. For example, you can say to your child, "I see a couch. Couch. What letter does *couch* begin with?" (Make sure to emphasize the first letter when teaching beginning sounds.)

Let's review:

The **A** says /ă/, as in **apple**, ant, act.
The **B** says **baby**, big, box.

C

Now we are going to learn the letter **C** sound.
The letter **C** is called a consonant.
The **C** says **cat**, cook, cot.
Can you think of any other words that begin with the letter **C**?

Here are some C words to help you along: cook, cot, candy, car, cane, candle, cake, cow, cup, coat, corn, cob, comb, camp.

cat

LETTER D

BEFORE THE LESSON: Start by introducing the upper- and lowercase letter cards, saying, "This is the letter **D**. See how the letter is big and little? The big letter is called the uppercase letter, and the little letter is called the lowercase letter. They are both the same letter, and they both have the same sound."

AFTER THE LESSON: At any time during the day, you can reinforce the letters you have taught. For example, you can say to your child, "I see a dad. Dad. What letter does *dad* begin with?" (Make sure to emphasize the first letter when teaching beginning sounds.)

Let's review:

The **A** says /ă/, as in **apple**, ant, act.
The **B** says **baby**, big, box.
The **C** says **cat**, cook, cot.

D

Now we are going to learn the letter **D** sound.
The letter **D** is called a consonant.
The **D** says **dog**, dish, dad.
Can you think of any other words that begin with the letter **D**?

*Here are some **D** words to help you along: duck, door, digger, dog, desk, doll, deer, dice, deep, dish, dig, door.*

dog

LETTER E

BEFORE THE LESSON: Start by introducing the upper- and lowercase letter cards, saying, "This is the letter **E**. See how the letter is big and little? The big letter is called the uppercase letter, and the little letter is called the lowercase letter. They are both the same letter, and they both have the same sound."

AFTER THE LESSON: At any time during the day, you can reinforce the letters you have taught. For example, you can say to your child, "I see an egg. Egg. What letter does *egg* begin with?" (Make sure to emphasize the first letter when teaching beginning sounds.)

E followed by R or W doesn't make the short-E (ĕ) sound (though there are always exceptions to this rule). You don't need to point this out to your child now, but you, as the parent, need to know that the words her *and* grew *don't make the /ĕ/ sound. The letter E followed by the letter L sounds like "el"; therefore, children think it is the letter L because that's what they hear: elephant, elk, elm. I therefore try to avoid words with the E followed by the L when the child is just beginning to spell.*

Let's review:

The **A** says /ă/, as in **apple**, ant, act.
The **B** says **baby**, big, box.
The **C** says **cat**, cook, cot.
The **D** says **dog**, dish, dad.

E

Now we are going to learn the letter **E** sound.
The letter **E** is called a vowel.
The **E** says /ĕ/, as in **egg**, extra, end.
Can you think of any other words that begin with the /ĕ/ sound?

*Here are some /ĕ/ words to help you along: etch, extra, empty, emerald, engine, envelope, every, exercise.

LETTER F

<u>BEFORE THE LESSON</u>: Start by introducing the upper- and lowercase letter cards, saying, "This is the letter **F**. See how the letter is big and little? The big letter is called the uppercase letter, and the little letter is called the lowercase letter. They are both the same letter, and they both have the same sound."

<u>AFTER THE LESSON</u>: At any time during the day, you can reinforce the letters you have taught. For example, you can say to your child, "I see a fish. Fish. What letter does *fish* begin with?" (Make sure to emphasize the first letter when teaching beginning sounds.)

Let's review:

The **A** says /ă/, as in **apple**, ant, act.
The **B** says **baby**, big, box.
The **C** says **cat**, cook, cot.
The **D** says **dog**, dish, dad.
The **E** says /ĕ/, as in **egg**, extra, end.

F

Now we are going to learn the letter **F** sound.
The letter **F** is called a consonant.
The letter **F** says **fish**, fat, fight.
Can you think of any other words that begin with the letter **F**?

Here are some F words to help you along: five, fork, fix, fight, food, fingers, foot, four, fish, fan, fast, fox, fence, find, feet.

LETTER G

BEFORE THE LESSON: Start by introducing the upper- and lowercase letter cards, saying, "This is the letter **G**. See how the letter is big and little? The big letter is called the uppercase letter, and the little letter is called the lowercase letter. They are both the same letter, and they both have the same sound."

AFTER THE LESSON: At any time during the day, you can reinforce the letters you have taught. For example, you can say to your child, "I see a girl. Girl. What letter does *girl* begin with?" (Make sure to emphasize the first letter when teaching beginning sounds.)

Let's review:

The **A** says /ă/, as in **apple**, ant, act.
The **B** says **baby**, big, box.
The **C** says **cat**, cook, cot.
The **D** says **dog**, dish, dad.
The **E** says /ĕ/, as in **egg**, extra, end.
The **F** says **fish**, fat, fight.

G

Now we are going to learn the letter **G** sound.
The letter **G** is called a consonant.
The **G** says **go**, goat, gold.
Can you think of any other words that begin with the letter **G**?

go

*Here are some **G** words to help you along: good, girl, gas, gone, gum, ghost, game, gumball, got, good.*

LETTER H

<u>BEFORE THE LESSON</u>: Start by introducing the upper- and lowercase letter cards, saying, "This is the letter **H**. See how the letter is big and little? The big letter is called the uppercase letter, and the little letter is called the lowercase letter. They are both the same letter, and they both have the same sound."

<u>AFTER THE LESSON</u>: At any time during the day, you can reinforce the letters you have taught. For example, you can say to your child, "I see a house. House. What letter does *house* start with?" (Make sure to emphasize the first letter when teaching beginning sounds.)

Let's review:

The **A** says /ă/, as in **apple**, ant, act.
The **B** says **baby**, big, box.
The **C** says **cat**, cook, cot.
The **D** says **dog**, dish, dad.
The **E** says /ĕ/, as in **egg**, extra, end.
The **F** says **fish**, fat, fight.
The **G** says **go**, goat, gold.

H

Now we are going to learn the letter **H** sound.
The letter **H** is called a consonant.
The letter **H** says **house**, hot, hand.
Can you think of any other words that begin with the letter **H**?

house

*Here are some **H** words to help you along: horse, hose, home, horn, hook, hat, heart, ham, heat, hop, hope.*

LETTER I

<u>BEFORE THE LESSON</u>: Start by introducing the upper- and lowercase letter cards, saying, "This is the letter **I**. See how the letter is big and little? The big letter is called the uppercase letter, and the little letter is called the lowercase letter. They are both the same letter, and they both have the same sound."

<u>AFTER THE LESSON</u>: At any time during the day, you can reinforce the letters you have taught. For example, you can say to your child, "I see an igloo. Igloo. What letter does *igloo* start with?" (Make sure to emphasize the first letter when teaching beginning sounds.)

I followed by R doesn't make the short-I (ĭ) sound (though there are always exceptions to this rule). You don't need to point this out to your child now, but you, as the parent, need to know that* bird *and* skirt *don't make the /ĭ/ sound.

Let's review:

The **A** says /ă/, as in **apple**, ant, act.
The **B** says **baby**, big, box.
The **C** says **cat**, cook, cot.
The **D** says **dog**, dish, dad.
The **E** says /ĕ/, as in **egg**, extra, end.
The **F** says **fish**, fat, fight.
The **G** says **go**, goat, gold.
The **H** says **house**, hot, hand.

I

Now we are going to learn the letter **I** sound.
The letter **I** is called a vowel.
The **I** says /ĭ/, as in **itch**, ink, if.
Can you think of any other words that begin with the /ĭ/ sound?

itch

Here are some /ĭ/ words to help you along: if, it, inch, icky, in, iguana, Indiana, Illinois, igloo, infant, invitation.

LETTER J

BEFORE THE LESSON: Start by introducing the upper- and lowercase letter cards, saying, "This is the letter **J**. See how the letter is big and little? The big letter is called the uppercase letter, and the little letter is called the lowercase letter. They are both the same letter, and they both have the same sound."

AFTER THE LESSON: At any time during the day, you can reinforce the letters you have taught. For example, you can say to your child, "I see a jar of jam. Jam. What letter does *jam* begin with?" (Make sure to emphasize the first letter when teaching beginning sounds.)

Let's review:

The **A** says /ă/, as in **apple**, ant, act.
The **B** says **baby**, big, box.
The **C** says **cat**, cook, cot.
The **D** says **dog**, dish, dad.
The **E** says /ĕ/, as in **egg**, extra, end.
The **F** says **fish**, fat, fight.
The **G** says **go**, goat, gold.
The **H** says **house**, hot, hand.
The **I** says /ĭ/, as in **itch**, ink, if.

J

| jump |

Now we are going to learn the letter **J** sound.
The letter **J** is called a consonant.
The **J** says **jump**, jet, jug.
Now we are going to think of words that begin with the letter **J**.
Can you think of any other words that begin with the letter **J**?

Here are some J words to help you along: jar, jacket, jacks, jeep, jam, jelly, junk, juice, jelly, jellyfish.

LETTER K

<u>BEFORE THE LESSON</u>: Start by introducing the upper- and lowercase letter cards, saying, "This is the letter **K**. See how the letter is big and little? The big letter is called the uppercase letter, and the little letter is called the lowercase letter. They are both the same letter, and they both have the same sound."

<u>AFTER THE LESSON</u>: At any time during the day, you can reinforce the letters you have taught. For example, you can say to your child, "I see a kite. Kite. What letter does *kite* begin with?" (Make sure to emphasize the first letter when teaching beginning sounds.)

Let's review:

The **A** says /ă/, as in **apple**, ant, act.
The **B** says **baby**, big, box.
The **C** says **cat**, cook, cot.
The **D** says **dog**, dish, dad.
The **E** says /ĕ/, as in **egg**, extra, end.
The **F** says **fish**, fat, fight.
The **G** says **go**, goat, gold.
The **H** says **house**, hot, hand.
The **I** says /ĭ/, as in **itch**, ink, if.
The **J** says **jump**, jet, jug.

K

Now we are going to learn the letter **K** sound.
The letter **K** is called a consonant.
The letter **K** says **kite**, kit, key.
Can you think of any words that begin with the letter **K**?

kite

*Here are some **K** words to help you along: kitchen, kitten, kangaroo, kick, king, key, Kansas.*

LETTER L

<u>BEFORE THE LESSON</u>: Start by introducing the upper- and lowercase letter cards, saying, "This is the letter **L**. See how the letter is big and little? The big letter is called the uppercase letter, and the little letter is called the lowercase letter. They are both the same letter, and they both have the same sound."

<u>AFTER THE LESSON</u>: At any time during the day, you can reinforce the letters you have taught. For example, you can say to your child, "I see a leaf. Leaf. What letter does *leaf* start with?" (Make sure to emphasize the first letter when teaching beginning sounds.)

Let's review:

The **A** says /ă/, as in **apple**, ant, act.
The **B** says **baby**, big, box.
The **C** says **cat**, cook, cot.
The **D** says **dog**, dish, dad.
The **E** says /ĕ/, as in **egg**, extra, end.
The **F** says **fish**, fat, fight.
The **G** says **go**, goat, gold.
The **H** says **house**, hot, hand.
The **I** says /ĭ/, as in **itch**, ink, if.
The **J** says **jump**, jet, jug.
The **K** says **kite**, kit, key.

L

lollipop

Now we are going to learn the letter **L** sound.
The letter **L** is called a consonant.
The **L** says **lollipop**, lock, leg.
Can you think of any other words that begin with the letter **L**?

*Here are some **L** words to help you along: limp, leg, list, laugh, leaf, leaves, lips, log, letter.*

LETTER M

<u>BEFORE THE LESSON</u>: Start by introducing the upper- and lowercase letter cards, saying, "This is the letter **M**. See how the letter is big and little? The big letter is called the uppercase letter, and the little letter is called the lowercase letter. They are both the same letter, and they both have the same sound."

<u>AFTER THE LESSON</u>: At any time during the day, you can reinforce the letters you have taught. For example, you can say to your child, "I see a mouse. Mouse. What letter does *mouse* begin with?" (Make sure to emphasize the first letter when teaching beginning sounds.)

Let's review:

The **A** says /ă/, as in **apple**, ant, act.
The **B** says **baby**, big, box.
The **C** says **cat**, cook, cot.
The **D** says **dog**, dish, dad.
The **E** says /ĕ/, as in **egg**, extra, end.
The **F** says **fish**, fat, fight.
The **G** says **go**, goat, gold.
The **H** says **house**, hot, hand.
The **I** says /ĭ/, as in **itch**, ink, if.
The **J** says **jump**, jet, jug.
The **K** says **kite**, kit, key.
The **L** says **lollipop**, lock, leg.

M

Now we are going to learn the letter **M** sound.
The letter **M** is called a consonant.
The letter **M** says **mom**, monkey, moon.
Can you think of any other words that begin with the letter **M**?

mom

*Here are some **M** words to help you along: man, mouse, mice, mop, mat, mask, make, milk, mitten, map, match.*

LETTER N

<u>BEFORE THE LESSON</u>: Start by introducing the upper- and lowercase letter cards, saying, "This is the letter **N**. See how the letter is big and little? The big letter is called the uppercase letter, and the little letter is called the lowercase letter. They are both the same letter, and they both have the same sound."

<u>AFTER THE LESSON</u>: At any time during the day, you can reinforce the letters you have taught. For example, you can say to your child, "I see a nose. Nose. What letter does *nose* begin with?" (Make sure to emphasize the first letter when teaching beginning sounds.)

Let's review:

The **A** says /ă/, as in **apple**, ant, act.
The **B** says **baby**, big, box.
The **C** says **cat**, cook, cot.
The **D** says **dog**, dish, dad.
The **E** says /ĕ/, as in **egg**, extra, end.
The **F** says **fish**, fat, fight.
The **G** says **go**, goat, gold.
The **H** says **house**, hot, hand.
The **I** says /ĭ/, as in **itch**, ink, if.
The **J** says **jump**, jet, jug.
The **K** says **kite**, kit, key.
The **L** says **lollipop**, lock, leg.
The **M** says **mom**, monkey, moon.

N

Now we are going to learn the letter **N** sound.
The letter **N** is called a consonant.
The **N** says **no**, nut, net.
Can you think of any other words that begin with the letter **N**?

no

*Here are some N words to help you along: nest, net, nine, nail, nose, needle, newspaper, nap.

LETTER O

<u>BEFORE THE LESSON</u>: Start by introducing the upper- and lowercase letter cards, saying, "This is the letter **O**. See how the letter is big and little? The big letter is called the uppercase letter, and the little letter is called the lowercase letter. They are both the same letter, and they both have the same sound."

<u>AFTER THE LESSON</u>: At any time during the day, you can reinforce the letters you have taught. For example, you can say to your child, "I see an ostrich. Ostrich. What letter does *ostrich* begin with?" (Make sure to emphasize the first letter when teaching beginning sounds.)

O followed by R, Y, U, or W doesn't make the short-O (ŏ) sound (though there are always exceptions to this rule). You don't need to point this out to your child now, but you, as the parent, need to know that **for, boy, cloud,** *and* **cow** *don't make the /ŏ/ sound.*

Let's review:

The **A** says /ă/, as in **apple**, ant, act.
The **B** says **baby**, big, box.
The **C** says **cat**, cook, cot.
The **D** says **dog**, dish, dad.
The **E** says /ĕ/, as in **egg**, extra, end.
The **F** says **fish**, fat, fight.
The **G** says **go**, goat, gold.
The **H** says **house**, hot, hand.
The **I** says /ĭ/, as in **itch**, ink, if.
The **J** says **jump**, jet, jug.
The **K** says **kite**, kit, key.
The **L** says **lollipop**, lock, leg.
The **M** says **mom**, monkey, moon.
The **N** says **no**, nut, net.

O

Now we are going to learn the letter **O** sound.
The letter **O** is called a vowel.
The **O** says /ŏ/, as in **octopus**, on, odd.
Can you think of any other words that begin with the /ŏ/ sound?

octopus

*Here are some /ŏ/ words to help you along: opposite, ostrich, opera, Oliver, olives, omelet, otter, opposite, October.

LETTER P

BEFORE THE LESSON: Start by introducing the upper- and lowercase letter cards, saying, "This is the letter **P**. See how the letter is big and little? The big letter is called the uppercase letter, and the little letter is called the lowercase letter. They are both the same letter, and they both have the same sound."

AFTER THE LESSON: At any time during the day, you can reinforce the letters you have taught. For example, you can say to your child, "I see a potato. Potato. What letter does *potato* begin with?" (Make sure to emphasize the first letter when teaching beginning sounds.)

Let's review:

The **A** says /ă/, as in **apple**, ant, act.
The **B** says **baby**, big, box.
The **C** says **cat**, cook, cot.
The **D** says **dog**, dish, dad.
The **E** says /ĕ/, as in **egg**, extra, end.
The **F** says **fish**, fat, fight.
The **G** says **go**, goat, gold.
The **H** says **house**, hot, hand.
The **I** says /ĭ/, as in **itch**, ink, if.
The **J** says **jump**, jet, jug.
The **K** says **kite**, kit, key.
The **L** says **lollipop**, lock, leg.
The **M** says **mom**, monkey, moon.
The **N** says **no**, nut, net.
The **O** says /ŏ/, as in **octopus**, otter, olive.

P

Now we are going to learn the letter **P** sound.
The letter **P** is called a consonant.
The **P** says **popsicle**, pot, pin.
Can you think of any other words that begin with the letter **P**?

popsicle

*Here are some **P** words to help you along: pinch, point, pick, pen, pinch, pie, play.*

LETTER Q

BEFORE THE LESSON: Start by introducing the upper- and lowercase letter cards, saying, "This is the letter **Q**. See how the letter is big and little? The big letter is called the uppercase letter, and the little letter is called the lowercase letter. They are both the same letter, and they both have the same sound."

AFTER THE LESSON: At any time during the day, you can reinforce the letters you have taught. For example, you can say to your child, "I see a quilt. Quilt. What letter does *quilt* begin with?" (Make sure to emphasize the first letter when teaching beginning sounds.)

Let's review:

The **A** says /ă/, as in **apple**, ant, act.
The **B** says **baby**, big, box.
The **C** says **cat**, cook, cot.
The **D** says **dog**, dish, dad.
The **E** says /ĕ/, as in **egg**, extra, end.
The **F** says **fish**, fat, fight.
The **G** says **go**, goat, gold.
The **H** says **house**, hot, hand.
The **I** says /ĭ/, as in **itch**, ink, if.
The **J** says **jump**, jet, jug.
The **K** says **kite**, kit, key.
The **L** says **lollipop**, lock, leg.
The **M** says **mom**, monkey, moon.
The **N** says **no**, nut, net.
The **O** says /ŏ/, as in **octopus**, otter, olive.
The **P** says **popsicle**, pot, pin.

Q

queen

Now we are going to learn the letter **Q** sound.
The letter **Q** is called a consonant.
The letter **Q** is a special consonant because it is the only letter that doesn't make a sound on its own and therefore, can't be written on its own. The letter **Q** is always followed by the vowel letter **U**. We say that the letters **Q** and **U** are married. Together, they make the /**kw**/ sound.
The **Q** says **queen**, quit, question.
Can you think of any other words that begin with the letter **Q**?

*Here are some **Q** words to help you along: quiet, quack, quilt.*

LETTER R

<u>BEFORE THE LESSON</u>: Start by introducing the upper- and lowercase letter cards, saying, "This is the letter **R**. See how the letter is big and little? The big letter is called the uppercase letter, and the little letter is called the lowercase letter. They are both the same letter, and they both have the same sound."

<u>AFTER THE LESSON</u>: At any time during the day, you can reinforce the letters you have taught. For example, you can say to your child, "I see a rabbit. Rabbit. What letter does *rabbit* begin with?" (Make sure to emphasize the first letter when teaching beginning sounds.)

Let's review:

The **A** says /ă/, as in **apple**, ant, act.
The **B** says **baby**, big, box.
The **C** says **cat**, cook, cot.
The **D** says **dog**, dish, dad.
The **E** says /ĕ/, as in **egg**, extra, end.
The **F** says **fish**, fat, fight.
The **G** says **go**, goat, gold.
The **H** says **house**, hot, hand.
The **I** says /ĭ/, as in **itch**, ink, if.
The **J** says **jump**, jet, jug.
The **K** says **kite**, kit, key.
The **L** says **lollipop**, lock, leg.
The **M** says **mom**, monkey, moon.
The **N** says **no**, nut, net.
The **O** says /ŏ/, as in **octopus**, otter, olive.
The **P** says **popsicle**, pot, pin.
The **Q** says **queen**, quit, question.

R

Now we are going to learn the letter **R** sound.
The letter **R** is called a consonant.
The **R** says **run**, rabbit, roll.
Can you think of any other words that begin with the letter **R**?

run

Here are some **R words to help you along: rich, race, reach, refrigerator, recipe, recite, recycle.*

LETTER S

<u>BEFORE THE LESSON</u>: Start by introducing the upper- and lowercase letter cards, saying, "This is the letter **S**. See how the letter is big and little? The big letter is called the uppercase letter, and the little letter is called the lowercase letter. They are both the same letter, and they both have the same sound."

<u>AFTER THE LESSON</u>: At any time during the day, you can reinforce the letters you have taught. For example, you can say to your child, "I see a soccer ball. Soccer. What letter does *soccer* begin with?" (Make sure to emphasize the first letter when teaching beginning sounds.)

Let's review:

The **A** says /ă/, as in **apple**, ant, act.
The **B** says **baby**, big, box.
The **C** says **cat**, cook, cot.
The **D** says **dog**, dish, dad.
The **E** says /ĕ/, as in **egg**, extra, end.
The **F** says **fish**, fat, fight.
The **G** says **go**, goat, gold.
The **H** says **house**, hot, hand.
The **I** says /ĭ/, as in **itch**, ink, if.
The **J** says **jump**, jet, jug.
The **K** says **kite**, kit, key.
The **L** says **lollipop**, lock, leg.
The **M** says **mom**, monkey, moon.
The **N** says **no**, nut, net.
The **O** says /ŏ/, as in **octopus**, otter, olive.
The **P** says **popsicle**, pot, pin.
The **Q** says **queen**, quit, question.
The **R** says **run**, rabbit, roll.

S

Now we are going to learn the letter **S** sound.
The letter **S** is called a consonant.
The **S** says **so**, say, sorry.
Can you think of any other words that begin with the letter **S**?

SO

Here are some S words to help you along: smoke, stack, simple, sack, sausage, snake, soda, smile, stamp, soap, seal, sock.

LETTER T

<u>BEFORE THE LESSON</u>: Start by introducing the upper- and lowercase letter cards, saying, "This is the letter **T**. See how the letter is big and little? The big letter is called the uppercase letter, and the little letter is called the lowercase letter. They are both the same letter, and they both have the same sound."

<u>AFTER THE LESSON</u>: At any time during the day, you can reinforce the letters you have taught. For example, you can say to your child, "I see a teacher. Teacher. What letter does *teacher* begin with?" (Make sure to emphasize the first letter when teaching beginning sounds.)

Let's review:

The **A** says /ă/, as in **apple**, ant, act.
The **B** says **baby**, big, box.
The **C** says **cat**, cook, cot.
The **D** says **dog**, dish, dad.
The **E** says /ĕ/, as in **egg**, extra, end.
The **F** says **fish**, fat, fight.
The **G** says **go**, goat, gold.
The **H** says **house**, hot, hand.
The **I** says /ĭ/, as in **itch**, ink, if.
The **J** says **jump**, jet, jug.
The **K** says **kite**, kit, key.
The **L** says **lollipop**, lock, leg.
The **M** says **mom**, monkey, moon.
The **N** says **no**, nut, net.
The **O** says /ŏ/, as in **octopus**, otter, olive.
The **P** says **popsicle**, pot, pin.
The **Q** says **queen**, quit, question.
The **R** says **run**, rabbit, roll.
The **S** says **so**, say, sorry.

T

Now we are going to learn the letter **T** sound.
The letter **T** is called a consonant.
The **T** says **top**, take, time.
Can you think of any other words that begin with the letter **T**?

*Here are some **T** words to help you along: tomorrow, toe, turtle, table, tread, ten, take, took, tub, two, tire, tie, tired.*

LETTER U

BEFORE THE LESSON: Start by introducing the upper- and lowercase letter cards, saying, "This is the letter **U**. See how the letter is big and little? The big letter is called the uppercase letter, and the little letter is called the lowercase letter. They are both the same letter, and they both have the same sound."

AFTER THE LESSON: At any time during the day, you can reinforce the letters you have taught. For example, you can say to your child, "I see an umbrella. Umbrella. What letter does *umbrella* begin with?" (Make sure to emphasize the first letter when teaching beginning sounds.)

U followed by R and Y don't make the short-U (ŭ) sound (though there are always exceptions to this rule). You don't need to point this out to your child now, but you, as the parent, need to know that words such as **buy**, **pour**, *and* **fur** *don't make the /ŭ/ sound.*

Let's review:

The **A** says /ă/, as in **apple**, ant, act.
The **B** says **baby**, big, box.
The **C** says **cat**, cook, cot.
The **D** says **dog**, dish, dad.
The **E** says /ĕ/, as in **egg**, extra, end.
The **F** says **fish**, fat, fight.
The **G** says **go**, goat, gold.
The **H** says **house**, hot, hand.
The **I** says /ĭ/, as in **itch**, ink, if.
The **J** says **jump**, jet, jug.
The **K** says **kite**, kit, key.
The **L** says **lollipop**, lock, leg.
The **M** says **mom**, monkey, moon.
The **N** says **no**, nut, net.
The **O** says /ŏ/, as in **octopus**, on, odd.
The **P** says **popsicle**, pot, pin.
The **Q** says **queen**, quit, question.
The **R** says **run**, rabbit, roll.
The **S** says **so**, say, sorry.
The **T** says **top**, take, time.

U

Now we are going to learn the letter U sound.
The letter U is called a vowel.
The **U** says /ŭ/, as in **up**, us, under.
Can you think of any other words that begin with the /ŭ/ sound?

up

*Here are some /ŭ/ words to help you along: unzip, underwear, underground, underline, umbrella, ugly, unhappy.

LETTER V

BEFORE THE LESSON: Start by introducing the upper- and lowercase letter cards, saying, "This is the letter **V**. See how the letter is big and little? The big letter is called the uppercase letter, and the little letter is called the lowercase letter. They are both the same letter, and they both have the same sound."

AFTER THE LESSON: At any time during the day, you can reinforce the letters you have taught. For example, you can say to your child, "I see a violin. Violin. What letter does *violin* begin with?" (Make sure to emphasize the first letter when teaching beginning sounds.)

Let's review:

The **A** says /ă/, as in **apple**, ant, act.
The **B** says **baby**, big, box.
The **C** says **cat**, cook, cot.
The **D** says **dog**, dish, dad.
The **E** says /ĕ/, as in **egg**, extra, end.
The **F** says **fish**, fat, fight.
The **G** says **go**, goat, gold.
The **H** says **house**, hot, hand.
The **I** says /ĭ/, as in **itch**, ink, if.
The **J** says **jump**, jet, jug.
The **K** says **kite**, kit, key.
The **L** says **lollipop**, lock, leg.
The **M** says **mom**, monkey, moon.
The **N** says **no**, nut, net.
The **O** says /ŏ/, as in **octopus**, on, odd.
The **P** says **popsicle**, pot, pin.
The **Q** says **queen**, quit, question.
The **R** says **run**, rabbit, roll.
The **S** says **so**, say, sorry.
The **T** says **top**, take, time.
The **U** says /ŭ/, as in **up**, us, under.

V

Now we are going to learn the letter **V** sound.
The letter **V** is called a consonant.
The letter **V** says **van**, vase, vacuum.
Can you think of any other words that begin with the letter **V**?

*Here are some V words to help you along: vine, vest, volcano, violin, vixen, vapor, verb, vinegar, vegetable.

van

LETTER W

BEFORE THE LESSON: Start by introducing the upper- and lowercase letter cards, saying, "This is the letter **W**. See how the letter is big and little? The big letter is called the uppercase letter, and the little letter is called the lowercase letter. They are both the same letter, and they both have the same sound."

AFTER THE LESSON: At any time during the day, you can reinforce the letters you have taught. For example, you can say to your child, "I see water. Water. What letter does *water* begin with?" (Make sure to emphasize the first letter when teaching beginning sounds.)

Let's review:

The **A** says /ă/, as in **apple**, ant, act.
The **B** says **baby**, big, box.
The **C** says **cat**, cook, cot.
The **D** says **dog**, dish, dad.
The **E** says /ĕ/, as in **egg**, extra, end.
The **F** says **fish**, fat, fight.
The **G** says **go**, goat, gold.
The **H** says **house**, hot, hand.
The **I** says /ĭ/, as in **itch**, ink, if.
The **J** says **jump**, jet, jug.
The **K** says **kite**, kit, key.
The **L** says **lollipop**, lock, leg.
The **M** says **mom**, monkey, moon.
The **N** says **no**, nut, net.
The **O** says /ŏ/, as in **octopus**, on, odd.
The **P** says **popsicle**, pot, pin.
The **Q** says **queen**, quit, question.
The **R** says **run**, rabbit, roll.
The **S** says **so**, say, sorry.
The **T** says **top**, take, time.
The **U** says /ŭ/, as in **up**, us, under.
The **V** says **van**, vase, vacuum.

W

Now we are going to learn the letter **W** sound.
The letter **W** is called a consonant.
The **W** says **we**, wet, wig.
Can you think of any other words that begin with the letter **W**?

we

*Here are some **W** words to help you along: wall, worm, witch, wrestle, window, wow, went, week, weekend, web.*

LETTER X

<u>BEFORE THE LESSON</u>: Start by introducing the upper- and lowercase letter cards, saying, "This is the letter **X**. See how the letter is big and little? The big letter is called the uppercase letter, and the little letter is called the lowercase letter. They are both the same letter, and they both have the same sound."

<u>AFTER THE LESSON</u>: At any time during the day, you can reinforce the letters you have taught. For example, you can say to your child, "I see a box. Box. What letter does *box* end with?" (Make sure to emphasize the last letter sound when teaching the /ks/ sound.)

Let's review:

The **A** says /ă/, as in **apple**, ant, act.
The **B** says **baby**, big, box.
The **C** says **cat**, cook, cot.
The **D** says **dog**, dish, dad.
The **E** says /ĕ/, as in **egg**, extra, end.
The **F** says **fish**, fat, fight.
The **G** says **go**, goat, gold.
The **H** says **house**, hot, hand.
The **I** says /ĭ/, as in **itch**, ink, if.
The **J** says **jump**, jet, jug.
The **K** says **kite**, kit, key.
The **L** says **lollipop**, lock, leg.
The **M** says **mom**, monkey, moon.
The **N** says **no**, nut, net.
The **O** says /ŏ/, as in **octopus**, on, odd.
The **P** says **popsicle**, pot, pin.
The **Q** says **queen**, quit, question.
The **R** says **run**, rabbit, roll.
The **S** says **so**, say, sorry.
The **T** says **top**, take, time.
The **U** says /ŭ/, as in **up**, us, under.
The **V** says **van**, vase, vacuum.
The **W** says **we**, wet, wig.

X

Now we are going to learn the letter **X** sound.
The letter **X** is called a consonant.
The **X** is a special letter because words don't begin with this sound but they end with this sound. The **X** makes the sound /**ks**/.
The **X** says **box**, fox, fix.
Can you think of any other words that end with the letter **X**?

Here are some X words to help you along: max, six, sax, wax, mix.

LETTER Y

<u>BEFORE THE LESSON</u>: Start by introducing the upper- and lowercase letter cards, saying, "This is the letter **Y**. See how the letter is big and little? The big letter is called the uppercase letter, and the little letter is called the lowercase letter. They are both the same letter, and they both have the same sound."

<u>AFTER THE LESSON</u>: At any time during the day, you can reinforce the letters you have taught. For example, you can say to your child, "I see the yo-yo. Yo-Yo. What letter does *yo-yo* begin with?" (Make sure to emphasize the first letter when teaching beginning sounds.)

Let's review:

The **A** says /ă/, as in **apple**, ant, act.
The **B** says **baby**, big, box.
The **C** says **cat**, cook, cot.
The **D** says **dog**, dish, dad.
The **E** says /ĕ/, as in **egg**, extra, end.
The **F** says **fish**, fat, fight.
The **G** says **go**, goat, gold.
The **H** says **house**, hot, hand.
The **I** says /ĭ/, as in **itch**, ink, if.
The **J** says **jump**, jet, jug.
The **K** says **kite**, kit, key.
The **L** says **lollipop**, lock, leg.
The **M** says **mom**, monkey, moon.
The **N** says **no**, nut, net.
The **O** says /ŏ/, as in **octopus**, on, odd.
The **P** says **popsicle**, pot, pin.
The **Q** says **queen**, quit, question.
The **R** says **run**, rabbit, roll.
The **S** says **so**, say, sorry.
The **T** says **top**, take, time.
The **U** says /ŭ/, as in **up**, us, under.
The **V** says **van**, vase, vacuum.
The **W** says **we**, wet, wig.
The **X** says **box**, fox, fix.

Y

Now we are going to learn the letter **Y** sound.
The letter **Y** is called a consonant.
The **Y** says **yes**, yell, yard.
Can you think of any other words that begin with the letter **Y**?

yes

*Here are some **Y** words to help you along: yo-yo, yolk, yogurt, yawn, yoga, yesterday, yam, yikes, yacht, yield.*

LETTER Z

BEFORE THE LESSON: Start by introducing the upper- and lowercase letter cards, saying, "This is the letter **Z**. See how the letter is big and little? The big letter is called the uppercase letter, and the little letter is called the lowercase letter. They are both the same letter, and they both have the same sound."

AFTER THE LESSON: At any time during the day, you can reinforce the letters you have taught. For example, you can say to your child, "I see a zipper. Zipper. What letter does *zipper* begin with?" (Make sure to emphasize the first letter when teaching beginning sounds.)

Let's review:

The **A** says /ă/, as in **apple**, ant, act.
The **B** says **baby**, big, box.
The **C** says **cat**, cook, cot.
The **D** says **dog**, dish, dad.
The **E** says /ĕ/, as in **egg**, extra, end.
The **F** says **fish**, fat, fight.
The **G** says **go**, goat, gold.
The **H** says **house**, hot, hand.
The **I** says /ĭ/, as in **itch**, ink, if.
The **J** says **jump**, jet, jug.
The **K** says **kite**, kit, key.
The **L** says **lollipop**, lock, leg.
The **M** says **mom**, monkey, moon.
The **N** says **no**, nut, net.
The **O** says /ŏ/, as in **octopus**, on, odd.
The **P** says **popsicle**, pot, pin.
The **Q** says **queen**, quit, question.
The **R** says **run**, rabbit, roll.
The **S** says **so**, say, sorry.
The **T** says **top**, take, time.
The **U** says /ŭ/, as in **up**, us, under.
The **V** says **van**, vase, vacuum.
The **W** says **we**, wet, wig.
The **X** says **box**, fox, fix.
The **Y** says **yes**, yell, yard.

Z

Now we are going to learn the letter **Z** sound.
The letter **Z** is called a consonant.
The **Z** says **zip**, zoo, zebra.
Can you think of any other words that begin with the letter **Z**?

*Here are some **Z** words to help you along: zigzag, zero, zipper, zest, zap, zone, zilch, zoom.*

OPTIONAL/ADDITIONAL LETTER EXERCISES

The more you expose your child to each letter sound, the more opportunities his/her brain has to make the connection between each letter and its sound. These are additional quick letter exercises you can use throughout the day to reinforce any letter that you have already introduced. This is optional, although I do suggest that any time you have one minute, you try to reinforce the letter sounds that you have taught.

Letter/Sound Exercises

1. Play the sound game I Spy in the car.

   a. I spy an ant. What sound does *ant* begin with?
   b. I spy a bug. What sound does *bug* begin with?
   c. I spy a car. What sound does *car* begin with?
   d. I spy a house. What sound does *house* begin with?
   e. I spy grass. What sound does *grass* begin with?

2. Play the sound game I Spy in a store or at a restaurant.

   a. I spy a plate. What sound does *plate* begin with?
   b. I spy food. What sound does *food* begin with?
   c. I spy windows. What sound does *windows* begin with?

3. Play the sound game I Spy on a walk.

   a. Look, I see a garbage can. What sound does *garbage* begin with? (If your child responds with a correct response, great; move on to the next object. If your child responds with a wrong response, then model the correct response: "Listen, when I say *garbage,* I hear g…g…*garbage.* The /**g**/ sound is the letter **G**, like in **gold**." Make sure to always go back to the **key word** to remind your child of each letter sound. Next have your child think of something else that starts with a /**g**/ sound: goat, go, grab, get, give, glass…
   b. Now move on, whether your child was able to hear the beginning sound or not. The key is that the more you model the sounds, the faster your child will begin to have the correct response. It is okay if your child has the wrong response; just keep correcting him/her and modeling the correct sound.

STRETCH & CATCH

CHAPTER THREE

SHORT VOWELS

AMANDA MCNAMARA LOWE

BLUE TWL WORDS

the	not
of	we
a	can
and	said
to	an
in	do
is	if
you	up
it	out
he	so
was	go
me	see
she	no
for	my
on	am
are	put
as	here
I	us
at	set
be	but
or	end
by	big
but	off

DAILY READING

Your child is at the beginning stages of reading. During this stage of reading, your child is beginning to learn short-vowel words. Your child may not be ready to read a book independently yet, but will still learn a lot from an adult reading to him/her. Daily reading will therefore begin by the adult reading to the child. As the child moves through each chapter and begins to automatically identify TWL words, your child will slowly take over the reading and read to you. This will begin slowly. You will pick easy reader books, which weigh heavily on high-frequency words, repeated word patterns, and picture cues. When you come to a short-vowel word that your child has encountered within this chapter, stop and see if your child is able to identify it by using the Stretch & Catch Reading Strategy. If your child is not able to figure out the unknown word using this reading strategy, simply model the strategy for your child.

It is important to stop reading the print any time you come to a TWL word that your child has mastered. Let your child read the TWL word. The more your child encounters TWL words within print, the faster he/she will become at identifying them. You can encourage your child to look at the pictures within the book as another strategy for figuring out any unknown words; this is referred to as picture clues or cues. It is always okay for your child to have the wrong response while reading. It is important, however, for you to model the correct response for your child when he/she reads a word incorrectly or guesses a word. You may notice your child will guess words while reading. If this occurs with a short-vowel word, point to the word the child guessed and discuss the word. Point out the beginning, middle, and end sound to your child, then have him/her try to Stretch & Catch the word again, without guessing.

STRETCH & CATCH SHORT VOWELS

Short vowels have only one sound. The **A** says /ă/ as in **apple**, the **E** says /ĕ/ as in **egg**, the **I** says /ĭ/ as in **itch**, the **O** says /ŏ/ as in **octopus**, and the **U** says /ŭ/ as in **up**. All English words have vowels. You want to explain to your child in this chapter that all words must contain vowels. It is important for your child to be able to identify the vowels and consonants within words. After your child Stretches & Catches a word, you can reinforce this concept by asking your child which letters were consonants and which letter was the vowel within the word they spelled. For Features 2–13, the vowel will always be in the middle of the word.

The easiest way to teach short vowels is through teaching your child word families. Any time a short-vowel word has the same vowel and consonant ending, it is in the same word family. For example, the **at** word family consists of **cat, bat, sat, mat, fat, hat, pat,** and **rat.** We will be using word families to teach short vowels by Stretching & Catching them. There are also optional activities (Teaching Word Play and Teaching Rhyming) to reinforce the short-vowel feature at the end of this chapter.

Within each feature, you will be introducing a new word family for each lesson. You will do this by using the words provided for your child to Stretch & Catch. You may only want to introduce one word family at a time until your child begins to Stretch & Catch with 100% accuracy consistently. If one new word family is too easy, you may combine two or three lessons of word families and have your child compare the differences in the sounds and spellings. To challenge your child further, you can have him or her use the note cards to make all of the new words. If your child is having a difficult time mastering each lesson, it is important to use fewer words per week. You may want to use the same words several times during the week until your child masters them before adding any more words. Another way to reinforce the short-vowel features within this chapter is to use the optional lesson provided at the end of this chapter.

There are two templates that you can use to teach each word within the lessons. One template will be an adult-led Stretch & Catch, and the second will be a child-led Stretch & Catch. I suggest starting any lesson with the adult-led Stretch & Catch and then as soon as your child feels comfortable with Stretching & Catching as well as the feature you introduced, try to move to the child-led Stretch & Catch. It is important that your child begin Stretching & Catching on his/her own as soon as he/she is ready. If Stretching & Catching is too difficult for your child to do on his/her own, then continue using the adult-led template until your child feels comfortable Stretching & Catching with less support.

After your child has completed the words within each feature, you can use the assessment tool in Chapter One to see if he/she can move on to the next feature. Remember that 80% is mastery within each feature, but you may choose to stay in a feature for as long as your child needs. An assessment is only one tool in knowing if your child has mastered a feature. If you feel your child does well during your lessons, you can move on to the next feature even if he/she scores lower than an 80% on the assessment. A child's growth can be measured in many different ways, and you as the parent can decide when your child is ready to move to the next feature.

Stretching & Catching should be done three to five days per week. You can do this activity each time with one or more words. It is designed to fit within your schedule. You can take as long as your child needs for each lesson.

TEMPLATE FEATURES 2–6
(adult-led Stretch & Catch)

[Choose word]

Step 1: Say, "We are going to spell the word (**word**)."

Step 2: Now tell your child: "When I say (**first sound**) [sound the letter out and lift the first finger], (**vowel sound**) [sound the letter out and lift the second finger], (**third sound**) [sound the letter out and lift the third finger], do you see that I hear three sounds? So if I hear three sounds, there are three letters. Let's see what three letters we hear." [Leave your three fingers up.]

Step 3: Say the following: "When I say (**word**), I hear (**first sound**) [wriggle/point your first finger]. What letter is the (**first sound**) sound?" If your child says the letter, that is great. If your child gives an incorrect response, model by saying, "The (**first sound**) sound is (**letter**), like in (**key word**)." [Notice the use of the key word to model the correct response.]

Step 4: Sound out the first two sounds, stopping at the vowel sound. [Your fingers are still up.] "(**First sound**) [wriggle/point to first finger], (**vowel sound**) [wriggle/point to second finger]. The vowel sound is (**vowel sound**) [wriggle or point to the second finger]. What letter makes the (**vowel sound**) sound?" If your child gives the correct response, great. If not, model the correct response: "The (**vowel sound**) sound is the letter (**letter**) as in (**key word**)." [Notice the use of the key word to model the correct response.]

Step 5: Move on to the last sound. Sound out the entire word again. [Your fingers are still up.] "(**First sound**) [wriggle/point to first finger], (**vowel sound**) [wriggle/point to second finger], (**third sound**) [wriggle/point to third finger]." Emphasize the third sound by saying it again and wriggling/pointing to third finger: "(**Third** sound.) What is the last sound you hear in (**word**)?" If your child gets the answer correct, great; if not, model the correct response: "When I hear the word (**word**), I hear the (**third sound**) sound at the end. The (**third sound**) sound is a (**letter**), like in (**key word**)."

Step 6: Now put the three fingers down.

Step 7: Slowly Stretch the word again: "(**First sound**) [lift first finger], (**vowel sound**) [lift second finger], (**third sound**) [lift third finger]."

Step 8: Next, say, "(**Word**) is spelled (**spelling of word**) [wriggle or point to each finger as you spell the word]."

Step 9: Catch the word by saying it fast and pulling the three fingers back into a fist.

Step 10: When you first begin to Stretch & Catch words, you may want to say, "Did you see how I did that? That's how you Stretch & Catch words."

Optional: Finally, use the note cards to show your child the letters that make up the word, and have him/her manipulate the cards to make the new word.

Optional: Ask your child to identify the consonants and vowel in each word.

Optional: Use word cards to practice the Stretch & Catch Reading Strategy.

TEMPLATE FEATURES 2–6
(child-led Stretch & Catch)

Step 1: You say, "Can you Stretch & Catch the word (**word**)?"

Step 2: Your child will Stretch the word out and put one finger in the air per sound he/she says: "(**First sound**), (**short-vowel sound**), (**third sound**)."

Step 3: If your child is able to Stretch the word correctly, move to Step 4, otherwise move to the bullet point below.

- Say, "When I say (**first sound**) [sound the letter out and lift the first finger], (**vowel sound**) [sound the letter out and lift the second finger], (**third sound**) [sound the letter out and lift the third finger], do you see that I hear three sounds? What are the sounds I hear?" If the child answers with the correct three letters, great. Move to the next bullet point. If not, sound each letter out again while wriggling/pointing to the finger and saying each letter that corresponds with that sound: "(**First sound** and **first letter**)[wriggle/point to first finger], (**vowel sound** and **vowel letter**)[wriggle/point to second finger], (**third sound** and **third letter**) [wriggle/point to third finger]. Move to the next bullet point.
- (**Word**) is spelled (**spelling of word**)." Move to the next bullet point.
- Now have your child Stretch the word "(**first sound**), (**short-vowel sound**), (**third sound**)" (your child will lift one finger per sound). Move to Step 4.

Step 4: Now your child will look at his/her fingers and spell the word: "(**First letter**), (**vowel**), (**third letter**)."

Step 5: Now have your child Catch the word (say it all together quickly and bring his/her three fingers back into a fist). *Remember this is a technique that your child will need with the reading strategy.*

Optional: Finally, use the note cards to show your child the letters that make up the word, and have him/her manipulate the cards to make the new word.

Optional: Ask your child to identify the consonants and vowel in each word.

Optional: Use word cards to practice the Stretch & Catch Reading Strategy.

LESSONS FOR FEATURES 2-6

FEATURE 2 WORDS
Short A (ă)
2-1: **at**: cat, bat, sat, mat, fat, hat, pat, rat

2-2: **ag**: bag, rag, sag, wag, nag, lag, tag

2-3, **an**: can, fan, man, pan, ran, tan, van

2-4: **ap**: cap, lap, gap, map, nap, rap, yap, tap, zap

2-5: **ab**: cab, dab, jab, nab, lab, tab

2-6: **ad**: bad, dad, sad, lad, mad, pad, fad, rad, tad

2-7: **am**: dam, ham, ram, jam, Sam, bam, Cam, Pam, yam

FEATURE 3 WORDS
Short E (ĕ)
3-1: **et**: bet, get, let, met, net, pet, set, wet, vet, jet, yet

3-2: **en**: den, hen, men, ten, pen, Ben, Ken

3-3: **ed**: bed, fed, led, red, wed, Ted, Ned

3-4: **eg**: beg, peg, leg, keg, Meg

FEATURE 4 WORDS
Short I (ĭ)
4-1: **it**: bit, lit, sit, kit, wit, zit, fit, hit, pit

4-2: **id**: did, hid, lid, rid, kid, bid, Sid

4-3: **ig**: big, dig, fig, jig, pig, rig, wig, zig

4-4: **in**: bin, fin, pin, tin, din, win, sin, kin

4-5: **im**: dim, him, Jim, Kim, rim, Tim

FEATURE 5 WORDS
Short O (ŏ)
5-1: **op**: cop, hop, pop, mop, top, bop

5-2: **og**: bog, dog, fog, hog, jog, log

5-3: **ot**: cot, dot, got, hot, jot, lot, not, pot

5-4: **ob**: Bob, cob, job, rob, gob, mob, sob

FEATURE 6 WORDS
Short U (ŭ)
6-1: **ut**: rut, nut, hut, gut, cut, but

6-2: **ub**: cub, hub, rub, tub, pub, sub

6-3: **ug**: bug, dug, hug, jug, mug, rug, tug, lug

6-4: **um**: bum, gum, hum, sum, rum, yum

6-5: **un**: bun, fun, gun, run, sun, pun

EXAMPLE EXERCISE FEATURES 2–6
(adult-led)

cat

Step 1: Say, "We are going to spell the word **cat**."

Step 2: Now tell your child: "When I say /c/ [sound the letter out and lift the first finger], /ă/ [sound the letter out and lift the second finger], /t/ [sound the letter out and lift the third finger], do you see that I hear three sounds? So if I hear three sounds, there are three letters. Let's see what three letters we hear." Leave your three fingers up.

Step 3: Say the following: "When I say **cat**, I hear /c/ [wriggle/point to your first finger]. What letter is the /c/ sound?" If your child says the letter **C**, that is great. If your child gives an incorrect response, model by saying, "The /c/ sound is **C**, like in **cat**." (Notice the use of the key word to model the correct response.)

Step 4: Sound out the word again, stopping at the vowel sound. (Your fingers are still up.) "/c/ [wriggle/point to first finger], /ă/ [wriggle/point to second finger]. The vowel sound is /ă/ [wriggle or point to the second finger]. What letter makes the /ă/sound?" If your child gives the correct response, great. If not, model the correct response: "The /ă/ sound is the letter **A**, as in **apple**." [key word]

Step 5: Move on to the last sound. Sound out the word again. (Your fingers are still up.) "/c/ [wriggle/point to first finger], /ă/ [wriggle/point to second finger], /t/ [wriggle/point to third finger]." Emphasize the third sound while pointing to or wriggling the third finger again: "/t/. What is the last sound you hear in **cat**?" If your child gets the answer correct, great; if not, model the correct response: "When I hear the word **cat**, I hear the /t/ sound at the end. The /t/ sound is a **T**, like in **top** [key word]." Now put your three fingers down.

Step 6: Stretch the word again, putting a finger up in the air with each sound. Then look at your fingers and spell the word: "**Cat** is spelled **C** [wriggle/point to first finger], **A** [wriggle/point to second finger], **T** [wriggle/point to third finger]." Catch the word by saying it fast and pulling the three fingers back into a fist.

Step 7: When your child is first beginning to Stretch & Catch words, say, "Did you see how I did that? That's how you Stretch & Catch words."

Optional: Use the note cards to show your child the letters that make up the word, and have him/her manipulate the cards to make the new word.

Optional: Ask your child to identify the consonants and vowel in each word.

Optional: Use word cards to practice the Stretch & Catch Reading Strategy.

OPTIONAL ADDITIONAL LESSONS FOR FEATURES 2–6

WHAT IS WORD PLAY & RHYMING?

Word Play is a fun, interactive word game that your child can play using his or her lowercase letter note cards. Word Play encourages your child to manipulate the letter cards by changing only the first letter of a word from a word family. The goal is for your child to see how many words he/she can create by changing only the first letter of the word. You may use this activity with any feature/lesson that your child needs enrichment or reinforcement in. The more opportunities your child has to "play" with words by pulling the letters apart, putting the letters back together, and manipulating the letters, the more easily he/she will begin to Stretch & Catch words while reading.

While playing Word Play, point out to your child that the words they are making all rhyme. This activity also helps children understand rhyming. Rhyming is an important skill in reading because it helps children become aware of how important the sounds are within each word. It helps children understand that they can move or manipulate letters within words to make new words. This is an important skill not only for reading but also for writing. In writing, children will learn that they can use rhyme to help with spelling unknown words. For example, if your child knows how to spell **cat,** rhyming can help him/her discover that he/she can also spell **bat**, **sat**, and **mat**. Word Play helps children recognize that they can manipulate the letters within a word family to make many new words and that those new words rhyme.

Word Play can be used in several different ways. After teaching a feature lesson to your child, you can play Word Play with one word or with all of the words within that lesson. You can play Word Play by you choosing which letter will be placed in front of the word family as in the example below, or you can place the letter cards above the word family note cards and have your child pick which letter to place in front of the word family note cards. Either way, after your child manipulates each word, he/she will then Stretch & Catch it to discover what new word was made.

The activity can last as long as you want your child to play it.

WORD PLAY EXAMPLE

What you will need: at words needed from Feature 2, Lesson 1
Index cards: **c, b, f, h, m, p, r, a, t**

- Show your child the **a** and **t** note cards. Place the cards next to each other.
- Stretch & Catch the word **at**.
- Place the **c** in front of the **at**.
- Now Stretch & Catch the new word **cat**.
- Move the **c** away from the **at** and place the **b** in front of **at**.
- Stretch & Catch the new word **bat**.
- Move the **b** away from the **at** and place the **f** in front of **at**.
- Stretch & Catch the new word **fat**.
- Move the **f** away from the **at** and place the **h** in front of **at**.
- Stretch & Catch the new word **hat**.
- Move the **h** away from the **at** and place the **m** in front of **at**.
- Stretch & Catch the new word **mat**.

- Move the **m** away from the **at** and place the **p** in front of **at**.
- Stretch & Catch the new word **pat**.
- Move the **p** away from the **at** and place the **r** in front of **at**.
- Stretch & Catch the new word **rat**.

EXAMPLE OF THE SETUP FOR THE NOTE CARDS
FOR WORD PLAY WITH at WORDS

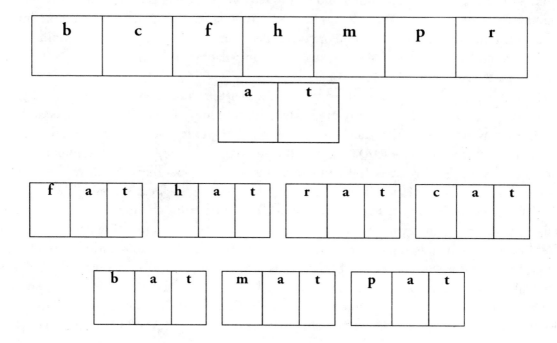

CHAPTER FOUR

BEGINNING AND ENDING BLENDS

AMANDA MCNAMARA LOWE

ORANGE TWL WORDS

all	went
call	from
has	let
first	then
into	talk
ask	walk
his	get
her	they
him	what
did	find
many	came
some	other
had	these
come	could
your	this
help	how
stop	over
know	away
with	little
down	them

DAILY READING

As your child begins learning the blend features, he/she is becoming a beginning reader. Your child is able to read beginning reading books and beginning-leveled books. It is important that your child begin reading to you daily, instead of you reading to him/her. Your child will still need to have a lot of support while reading, so make sure to sit next to him/her and help with any unknown words. If the unknown word contains a feature that you have taught your child, have your child use the Stretch & Catch Reading Strategy to try to figure it out. Encourage your child to also use picture and word clues (also called context clues) surrounding the unknown word while he/she is reading.

While your child is reading, have him/her point to each word as he/she reads the word. This is important because a lot of books at this reading level are pattern books that children memorize. If your child is pointing to each word as he/she reads, you know that your child understands where the words begin and end. This also makes the child look at the exact word he/she is reading at that moment. When the child guesses a word, you can remind him/her to *look* at the word and Stretch & Catch the word using the Stretch & Catch Reading Strategy.

STRETCH & CATCH
BEGINNING, ENDING, AND SPECIAL BLENDS

Blends are two letters that slide together at the beginning of a word. Beginning blends are divided into three groups: **S** blends, **R** blends, and **L** blends. It is important for your child to *hear* the blends in words so he/she can correctly spell the word. You also want to encourage your child to recognize any blends while reading and to use the Stretch & Catch Reading Strategy to figure out the new blend words.

After your child masters beginning blends, he/she will learn ending blends. Ending blends are the same as beginning blends in that they both slide two consonants together, except at the end of the word. At times, you will come upon words within your lessons that have both beginning and ending blends. These words consist of five letters. There is a specific Stretch & Catch template for this type of five-letter word. Please make sure to use it when teaching any lesson with both beginning and ending blends.

Special blends are taught at the end of this chapter after your child has mastered beginning and ending blends. Special blends are often referred to as pre-consonantal nasals. In this book, I will refer to them only as special blends, and you can simply call them ending blends when discussing them with your child. Special blends can be quite difficult for children to spell because the two consonants don't blend the same as beginning and ending blends do. In special blends, the first letter in the blend is often missed because it is a subtle sound combination. When children hear a word with a special blend (pre-consonantal nasal), the subtle first letter (**M** or **N**) is often missed due to the air passing through the nasal cavity in the mouth, while the second consonant takes over and absorbs the subtle nasal consonant (**M** or **N**) sound. Children often are unable to spell these words correctly because they do not hear the special blend (pre-consonantal nasal) and hear only the last letter within the blend.

You will introduce one or two blends per lesson, depending on your child's ability level. If introducing one blend is too easy for your child, introduce two blends. Each lesson can take as much or as little time as your child needs. Your child might master one lesson in one day, or it might take several weeks. There is no time schedule for your child's mastery of any feature. You need to teach your child at his/her instructional level.

When you feel your child has mastered any feature within this chapter, refer to the assessment tool in Chapter One and assess your child. Remember that 80% is mastery within the feature, but you may choose to stay in a feature for as long as your child needs. An assessment is only one tool in knowing if your child has mastered a feature. If you feel your child does well during your lessons, you can move on to the next feature even if he/she scored lower than 80% on the assessment. Remember that a child's growth can be measured many different ways and you can decide when your child is ready to move to the next feature.

This chapter also has one child-led Stretch & Catch template. I suggest starting any lesson with the adult-led Stretch & Catch and then, as soon as your child feels comfortable with Stretching & Catching as well as the new feature, try to move your child to the child-led Stretch & Catch. You will need to adapt this template to fit the needs of all of the different words your child will be Stretching & Catching. If Stretching & Catching is too difficult for your child to do on his/her own, then continue using the adult-led template until your child feels comfortable Stretching & Catching with less support.

TEMPLATE FEATURES 7–9
(adult-led Stretch & Catch)

Choose a word.

Step 1: Say, "We are going to spell the word (**word**)."

Step 2: Now tell your child, "When I say the word (**first sound**) [sound the letter out and lift first finger], (**second sound**) [sound the letter out and lift second finger], (**vowel sound**) [sound the letter out and lift third finger], (**fourth sound**) [sound the letter out and lift fourth finger] do you see that I hear four sounds? So if I hear four sounds, there are four letters. Did you hear the first two letters blending together?"

Step 3: With all four fingers still up, reinforce the blend sound by saying the first two sounds in the word again while wriggling only the first two fingers. Say, "I heard a (**first sound**), and then I heard (**second sound**). Do you hear how the first two letters blend together? That is called a beginning blend. We are going to blend two letters together before we get to our vowel."

Step 4: Say, "When I say (**word**), I hear (**first sound**). [With four fingers still up, wriggle or point to the first finger.] What letter makes the (**first sound**) sound?" If your child says the correct letter, that is great. If the child gives an incorrect response, model the correct response: "The (**first sound**) sound is the letter (**letter**), like in (**key word**)." (Notice the use of the key word to model the correct response.)

Step 5: Sound out the first two sounds, stopping at the second sound: "(**First sound**) (**second sound**). What letter makes the (**second sound**) sound? [With four fingers up, wriggle/point to the second finger.]" If the child gives the correct response, great. If not, model the correct response: "The (**second sound**) sound is the letter (**letter**), like in (**key word**)."

Step 6: With four fingers still up, Stretch the word out again, stopping at the vowel sound this time, wriggling/pointing to the third finger: "(**First sound**), (**second sound**), (**vowel sound**). What is the vowel sound you hear? (**vowel sound**)." If your child provides the correct answer, great. If not, model the correct response: "When I hear the word (**word**) [emphasize the vowel sound while pointing to the third finger], I hear the (**vowel sound**) sound. The (**vowel sound**) sound is the letter (**letter**) like in (**key word**)."

Step 7: Still holding four fingers up, Stretch the word out, "(**First sound**), (**second sound**), (**vowel sound**) (**fourth sound**) [using your fingers as a visual cue], then say, "What is the last sound you hear in (**word**)? [Make sure to emphasize the last sound.] (**Fourth sound.**)" If your child gives the correct answer, great. If not, model the correct response: "When I hear the word (**word**) [with four fingers up, point to the fourth finger], I hear the (**fourth sound**) sound at the end. The (**fourth sound**) sound is the letter (**letter**), like in (**key word**)."

Step 8: Now put all four fingers down. Slowly Stretch the word again, putting a finger in the air with each sound, "(**First sound**), (**second sound**), (**vowel sound**) (**fourth sound**)."

Step 9: Next, say, "(**Word**) is spelled (**spelling of word**) [wriggle/point to each finger as you spell the word]."

Step 10: Then catch the word, saying it all together quickly and bringing your four fingers back into a fist "(**word**)".

Optional: Finally, use the note cards to show your child the letters that make up the word, and have him/her manipulate the cards to make the new word.

Optional: Use word cards to practice the Stretch & Catch Reading Strategy.

TEMPLATE FEATURES 10–11
(adult-led Stretch & Catch)

Step 1: Say, "We are going to spell the word (**word**)."

Step 2: Now tell your child, "When I say the word (**first sound**) [sound the letter out and lift first finger], (**vowel sound**) [sound the letter out and lift second finger], (**third sound**) [sound the letter out and lift third finger], (**fourth sound**) [lift fourth finger] do you see that I hear four sounds? So if I hear four sounds, there are four letters. Did you hear the last two sounds blend together?" With all four fingers still up, reinforce the ending blend sound by saying the last two sounds in the word again while wriggling only the last two fingers, (**third sound**) (**fourth sound**) then say, "This word has an ending blend."

Step 3: With four fingers still up, say, "When I say (**word**), I hear (**first sound**) [wriggle/point to first finger]. What letter makes the (**first sound**) sound?" If your child says the correct letter, that is great. If your child gives an incorrect response, model the correct response: "The (**first sound**) sound is the letter (**letter**), like in (**key word**)." (Notice the use of the key word to model the correct response.)

Step 4: Sound out the first two sounds, stopping at the second sound: "(**First sound**), (**vowel sound**). What is the vowel sound you hear? (**Vowel sound**) [wriggle/point to second finger]. "If your child gives the correct response, great. If not, model the correct response: "The (**vowel sound**) sound is the letter (**letter**), like in (**key word**)."

Step 5: With four fingers still up, Stretch the word out again, stopping at the third sound this time, wriggling/pointing to the third finger: "(**First sound**), (**vowel sound**), (**third sound**). What is the third sound you hear?" Repeat the third sound. If your child provides the correct answer, great. If not, model the correct response: "When I hear the word (**word**) [emphasize the third sound while pointing to the third finger], I hear the (**third sound**) sound. The (**third sound**) sound is made by the letter (**letter**), like in (**key word**)."

Step 6: Still holding four fingers up, Stretch the word out, using your fingers as a visual cue, (**first sound**), (**vowel sound**), (**third sound**), (**fourth sound**), then say, "What is the last sound you hear in (**word**)?" Say the fourth sound, (**fourth sound**) making sure to emphasize it. If the child gives the correct answer, great. If not, model the correct response: "When I hear the word (**word**) [wriggle/point to the fourth finger], I hear the (**fourth sound**) sound at the end. The (**fourth sound**) sound is the letter (**letter**), like in (**key word**)."

Step 7: Now put all four fingers down. Slowly Stretch the word again, (**first sound**), (**vowel sound**), (**third sound**), (**fourth sound**) [putting a finger in the air with each sound].

Step 8: Next, say, "(**Word**) is spelled (**spelling of word**) [wriggle/point to each finger as you spell the word]."

Step 9: Then Catch the word by saying it all together quickly and bringing your four fingers back into a fist (**word**).

Optional: Finally, use the note cards to show your child the letters that make up the word, and have him/her manipulate the cards to make the new word.

Optional: Use word cards to practice the Stretch & Catch Reading Strategy.

TEMPLATE FEATURES 7–11
(adult-led Stretch & Catch)
*for words that have both a beginning blend and an ending blend

Step 1: Say, "We are going to spell the word (**word**)."

Step 2: Now tell your child, "When I say the word (**first sound**) [sound the letter out and lift first finger], (**second sound**) [sound the letter out and lift second finger], (**vowel sound**) [sound the letter out and lift third finger], (**fourth sound**) [sound the letter out and lift fourth finger], (**fifth sound**) [sound the letter out and lift fifth finger], do you see that I hear five sounds? So if I hear five sounds, there are five letters. Did you hear the first two letters blending together?" With all five fingers still up, reinforce the blend sound by saying the first two sounds in the word again while wriggling only the first two fingers (**first sound**) (**second sound**). Then say, "Did you also hear the last two sounds blend together?" With all five fingers still up, reinforce the ending blend sound by saying the last two sounds in the word again while wriggling only the last two fingers (**fourth sound**) (**fifth sound**). Say, "This word has two blends: a beginning and an ending blend."

Step 3: With all five fingers still up, say, "When I say (**word**), I hear (**first sound**). [Wriggle/point to first finger.] What letter makes the (**first sound**) sound?" If your child says the correct letter, that is great. If your child gives an incorrect response, model the correct response: "The (**first sound**) sound is the letter (**letter**), like in (**key word**)." (Notice the use of the key word to model the correct response.)

Step 4: Sound out the first two sounds, stopping at the second sound: "(**First sound**), (**second sound**) [wriggle/point to the second finger]. What letter makes the (**second sound**) sound?" If the child gives the correct response, great. If not, model the correct response: "The (**second sound**) sound is the letter (**letter**), like in (**key word**)."

Step 5: With five fingers still up, Stretch the word out again, stopping at the vowel sound this time, wriggling/pointing to the third finger: "(**First sound**), (**second sound**), (**vowel sound**). What is the vowel sound you hear? [Repeat the **vowel sound**.]" If your child provides the correct answer, great. If not, model the correct response: "When I hear the word (**word**) [emphasize the vowel sound while pointing to the third finger], I hear the (**vowel sound**) sound. The (**vowel sound**) sound is made by the letter (**letter**), like in (**key word**)."

Step 6: With five fingers still up, Stretch the word out again, stopping at the fourth sound, using your fingers as a visual cue, wriggling/pointing to each finger as you sound the letters out: "(**First sound**), (**second sound**), (**vowel sound**), (**fourth sound**), What is the fourth sound you hear? [Make sure to emphasize the fourth sound.]" If the child gives the correct answer, great. If not, model the correct response: "When I hear the word (**word**) [wriggle/point to the fourth finger], I hear the (**fourth sound**) sound. The (**fourth sound**) sound is the letter (**letter**), like in (**key word**)."

Step 7: Move on to the last sound. Stretch the word out, using your fingers as a visual cue: "(**First sound**), (**second sound**), (**vowel sound**), (**fourth sound**), (**fifth sound**). What is the last sound you hear in (**word**)?" [Make sure to emphasize the last sound.] "If your child gives the correct answer, great. If not, model the correct response: "When I hear the word (**word**) [wriggle/point to the fifth finger], I hear the (**fifth sound**) sound at the end. The (**fifth sound**) sound is the letter (**letter**), like in (**key word**)."

Step 8: Now put all five fingers down. Slowly Stretch the word, putting a finger in the air with each sound, "(**First sound**), (**second sound**), (**vowel sound**), (**fourth sound**), (**fifth sound**)."

Step 9: Next, say, "(**Word**) is spelled (**spelling of word**) [wriggle/point to each finger as you spell the word]."

Step 10: Then Catch the word, saying it all together quickly and bringing your five fingers back into a fist (**word**).

Optional: Finally, use the note cards to show your child the letters that make up the word, and have him/her manipulate the cards to make the new word.

Optional: Use word cards to practice the Stretch & Catch Reading Strategy.

TEMPLATE FEATURES 7–9
(child-led Stretch & Catch)

Step 1: Say, "Can you Stretch & Catch the word (**word**)?"

Step 2: Your child will Stretch the word out, putting one finger in the air per sound he/she says.

Step 3: If your child Stretched the word correctly, move to Step 4. If your child was unable to Stretch the word correctly, move to the bullet point below.

- Say, "When I say (**first sound**) [sounds the letter out and lift first finger], (**second sound**) [sound the letter out and lift second finger], (**vowel sound**) [sound the letter out and lift third finger], (**fourth sound**) [sound the letter out and lift fourth finger], do you see that I hear four sounds? What are the sounds I hear?" If the child provides the correct letters, great; move to the next bullet point. If not, again sound each letter out while wriggling/pointing to each finger and saying the letter that corresponds with that sound: "(**First sound** and **letter**), (**second sound** and **letter**), (**vowel sound** and **letter**), (**fourth sound** and **letter**)." Move to the next bullet point.
- Now have your child Stretch the same word out, putting one finger in the air per sound he/she says. Move to Step 4.

Step 4: Next, your child will look at his/her fingers and spell the word. [Make sure your child wriggles each finger as he/she says each sound.]

Step 5: Now have your child Catch the word, saying it all together quickly and bringing his/her fingers back into a fist. *Remember, this is a technique your child will need with the reading strategy.*

Optional: Finally, use the note cards to show your child the letters that make up the word, and have him/her manipulate the cards to make the new word.

Optional: Use word cards to practice the Stretch & Catch Reading Strategy.

TEMPLATE FEATURES 10–11
(child-led Stretch & Catch)

Step 1: Say, "Can you Stretch & Catch the word (**word**)?"

Step 2: Your child will Stretch the word out, putting one finger in the air per sound he/she says.

Step 3: If your child Stretched the word correctly, move to Step 4. If your child Stretched the word incorrectly, move to the bullet point below.

- Say, "When I say (**first sound**) [sound the letter out and lift first finger], (**vowel sound**) [sound the letter out and lift second finger], (**third sound**) [sound the letter out and lift third finger], (**fourth sound**) [sound the letter out and lift fourth finger], do you see that I hear four sounds? What are the sounds I hear?" If the child provides the correct four letters, great; move to the next bullet point. If not, then again sound each letter out while wriggling/pointing to a finger and saying the letter that corresponds with that sound: "(**First sound** and **letter**), (**short-vowel sound** and **letter**), (**third sound** and **letter**), (**fourth sound** and **letter**)."
- Now have your child Stretch the same word out, putting one finger in the air per sound he/she says.

Step 4: Next, your child will look at his/her fingers and spell the word.

Step 5: Now have your child Catch the word, saying it all together quickly and bringing his/her fingers back into a fist. *Remember, this is a technique that your child will need with the reading strategy.*

Optional: Finally, use the note cards to show your child the letters that make up the word, and have him/her manipulate the cards to make the new word.

Optional: Use word cards to practice the Stretch & Catch Reading Strategy.

LESSONS FOR FEATURES 7–11

FEATURE 7 WORDS
S Blends
7-1: **st**: stop, stem, stub, stun, step, stab, stag, Stan, stat
7-2: **sp**: spit, spun, spat, spin, span, spud, spam, sped
7-3: **sl**: slip, slop, slap, sled, slam, slat, slim, slit, slab
7-4: **sn**: snot, snip, snap, snag, snob, snub, snit, snug
7-5: **sk**: skim, skip, skit, skin, skid
7-6: **sw**: swam, swag, swig, swim, swop

FEATURE 8 WORDS
L Blends
8-1: **bl**: blob, blot, blab, bled, blub
8-2: **gl**: glam, glad, glob, glum, glib, glut
8-3: **fl**: flag, flop, flat, flip, flab, flan, flap, flax, fled
8-4: **cl**: clam, clip, clap, club, clan, clad, clog, clot
8-5: **pl**: plug, plus, plan, plum, plot

FEATURE 9 WORDS
R Blends
9-1: **tr**: trip, trim, trot, tram, trap, trod
9-2: **dr**: drip, drop, drum, drag, drab, drat, drib, drug
9-3: **br**: brad, brag, brim, bran, brat, bred
9-4: **fr**: frog, fret, frat, frit

FEATURE 10 WORDS
Ending Blends
10-1: **sk**: mask, task, ask, tusk, risk, flask
10-2: **st**: just, must, lost, best, list, pest, rust, blast
10-3: **ft**: raft, left, lift, gift, soft, craft, drift, sift, draft
10-4: **lf**: shelf, self, elf, golf, gulf

FEATURE 11 WORDS
Special Ending Blends
11-1: **mp**: lamp, jump, stamp, stump, lump, camp, ramp, damp, clamp
11-2: **nd**: hand, band, sand, land, stand, end, bend, send, tend, lend, blend
11-3: **nt**: mint, stint, lint, blunt, flint, plant, stunt, punt, runt
11-4: **nk**: skunk, bunk, junk, stink, pink, wink, drink, drunk, bank, sank, tank, wonk, trunk
11-5: **ng**: flung, cling, bling, sing, fling, king, sting, ding, ping, pong, song, tang, sang, sung, bung, lung

EXAMPLE EXERCISE FEATURES 7–9
(adult-led)

flag

Step 1: Say, "We are going to spell the word **flag**."

Step 2: Tell your child, "When I say the word /**f**/ [sound the letter out and lift first finger], /**l**/ [sound the letter out and lift second finger], /**ă**/ [sound the letter out and lift third finger], /**g**/ [sound the letter out and lift fourth finger], do you see that I hear four sounds? So if I hear four sounds, there are four letters. Did you hear the first two letters blending together?" With all four fingers still up, reinforce the blend sound by saying the first two sounds in the word again while wriggling only the first two fingers "/**f**/, /**l**/."

Step 3: Say, "I heard a /**f**/ and then I heard /**l**/. Do you hear how the first two letters blend together? That is called a beginning blend. We are going to blend two letters together before we get to our vowel."

Step 4: Say, "When I say **flag**, I hear /**f**/. [With four fingers still up, wriggle or point to the first finger.] What letter makes the /**f**/ sound?" If your child says the correct letter, that is great. If your child gives an incorrect response, model the correct response: "The /**f**/ sound is made by the letter **F**, like in **fish**." (Notice the use of the key word to model the correct response.)

Step 5: Sound out the first two sounds, "/**f**/, /**l**/" stopping at the second sound. Say, "What letter makes the /**l**/ sound? [With four fingers up, wriggle/point to the second finger.]" If the child gives the correct response, great. If not, model the correct response: "The /**l**/ sound is made by the letter **L**, like in **lollipop**."

Step 6: With four fingers still up, Stretch the word out again, stopping at the vowel sound this time while wriggling/pointing to the third finger: "/**f**/, /**l**/, /**ă**/. What is the vowel sound you hear? [Repeat the /**ă**/ sound.]" If your child provides the correct answer, great. If not, model the correct response: "When I hear the word **flag** [emphasize the vowel sound while pointing to the third finger], I hear the /**ă**/ sound. The /**ă**/ sound is made by the letter **A**, like in **apple**."

Step 7: Still holding four fingers up, Stretch the word out again, using your fingers as a visual cue: "/**f**/, /**l**/, /**ă**/, /**g**/. What is the last sound you hear in **flag**? [Make sure to emphasize the last sound] /**g**/." If your child gives the correct answer, great. If not, model the correct response: "When I hear the word **flag** [with four fingers up, point to the fourth finger], I hear the /**g**/ sound at the end. The /**g**/ sound is made by the letter **G**, like in **go**."

Step 8: Now put all four fingers down. Slowly Stretch the word again, putting a finger in the air with each sound, "/**f**/, /**l**/, /**ă**/, /**g**/".

Step 9: Next, say, "**Flag** is spelled **F-L-A-G** [wriggle or point to each finger as you spell the word]."

Step 10: Then Catch the word, saying it all together quickly and bringing your four fingers back into a fist "**flag**".

Optional: Finally, use the note cards to show your child the letters that make up the word, and have him/her manipulate the cards to make the new word.

Optional: Use word cards to practice the Stretch & Catch Reading Strategy.

EXAMPLE EXERCISE FEATURES 10–11
(adult-led)

mask

Step 1: Say, "We are going to spell the word **mask**."

Step 2: Tell your child, "When I say the word /**m**/ [sound the letter out and lift first finger], /**ă**/ [sound the letter out and lift second finger], /**s**/ [sound the letter out and lift third finger], /**k**/ [lift fourth finger], do you see that I hear four sounds? So if I hear four sounds, there are four letters. Did you hear the last two sounds blend together?" With all four fingers still up, reinforce the ending blend sound by saying the last two sounds in the word again while wriggling only the last two fingers "/**s**/, /**k**/". Say, "This word has an ending blend."

Step 3: With all four fingers still up, say, "When I say **mask**, I hear /**m**/. [Wriggle/ point to the first finger.] What letter makes the /**m**/ sound?" If your child says the correct letter, that is great. If your child gives an incorrect response, model the correct response: "The /**m**/ sound is made by the letter **M**, like in **mom**." (Notice the use of the key word to model the correct response.)

Step 4: Sound out the first two sounds, stopping at the second sound: "/**m**/, /**ă**/. What is the vowel sound you hear? [Repeat the vowel sound, wriggling/pointing to the second finger.]" If your child gives the correct response, great. If not, model the correct response: "The /**ă**/ sound is made by the letter **A,** like in **apple**."

Step 5: With four fingers still up, Stretch the word out again, stopping at the third sound this time, wriggling/pointing to the third finger: "/**m**/, /**ă**/, /**s**/. What is the third sound you hear? [Repeat the third sound.]" If your child provides the correct answer, great. If not, model the correct response: "When I hear the word **mask** [emphasize the third sound while pointing to the third finger], I hear the /**s**/ sound. The /**s**/ sound is made by the letter **S**, like in **so**."

Step 6: Still holding four fingers up, Stretch the word out, using your fingers as a visual cue: "/**m**/, /**ă**/, /**s**/, /**k**/. What is the last sound you hear in **mask**? [Make sure to emphasize the last sound.]" If your child gives the correct answer, great. If not, model the correct response: "When I hear the word **mask** [wriggle/point to the fourth finger], I hear the /**k**/ sound at the end. The /**k**/ sound is made by the letter **K**, like in **kite**."

Step 7: Now put all four fingers down. Slowly Stretch the word again, putting a finger in the air with each sound, "/**m**/, /**ă**/, /**s**/, /**k**/."

Step 8: Next, say, "**Mask** is spelled **M-A-S-K** [wriggle/point to each finger as you spell the word]."

Step 9: Then Catch the word, saying it all together quickly and bringing your four fingers back into a fist "**mask**".

Optional: Finally, use the note cards to show your child the letters that make up the word, and have him/her manipulate the cards to make the new word.

Optional: Use word cards to practice the Stretch & Catch Reading Strategy.

EXAMPLE EXERCISE FEATURES 7–11
(adult-led)

*for words that have both a beginning blend and an ending blend

drink

Step 1: Say, "We are going to spell the word **drink**."

Step 2: Tell your child, "When I say the word /**d**/ [sound the letter out and lift first finger], /**r**/ [sound the letter out and lift second finger], /ĭ/ [sound the letter out and lift third finger], /**n**/ [sound the letter out and lift fourth finger], /**k**/ [sound the letter out and lift fifth finger], do you see that I hear five sounds? So if I hear five sounds, there are five letters. Did you hear the first two letters blending together?" With all five fingers still up, reinforce the blend sound by saying the first two sounds in the word again while wriggling only the first two fingers: "/**d**/, /**r**/". " Did you also hear the last two sounds blend together?" With all five fingers still up, reinforce the ending blend sound by saying the last two sounds in the word again while wriggling only the last two fingers: "/**n**/, /**k**/. This word has two blends: a beginning and an ending blend."

Step 3: With five fingers still up, say, "When I say **drink**, I hear /**d**/. [Wriggle/point to the first finger.] What letter makes the /**d**/ sound?" If your child says the correct letter, that is great. If your child gives an incorrect response, model the correct response: "The /**d**/ sound is made by the letter **D,** like in **dog**." (Notice the use of the key word to model the correct response.)

Step 4: Sound out first two sounds, stopping at the second sound: "/**d**/, /**r**/. What letter makes the /**r**/ sound? [Wriggle/point to the second finger.]" If the child gives the correct response, great. If not, model the correct response: "The /**r**/ sound is the letter **R,** like in **run**."

Step 5: With five fingers still up, Stretch the word out again, stopping at the vowel sound this time, wriggling/pointing to the third finger: "/**d**/, /**r**/, /ĭ/. What is the vowel sound you hear? [Repeat the /ĭ/ sound.]" If your child provides the correct answer, great. If not, model the correct response: "When I hear the word **drink** [emphasize the vowel sound while pointing to the third finger], I hear the /ĭ/ sound. The /ĭ/ sound is made by the letter **I,** like in **itch**."

Step 6: With five fingers still up, Stretch the word out again, using your fingers as a visual cue, wriggling/pointing to each finger as you sound the letters out, stopping at the fourth sound: "/**d**/, /**r**/, /ĭ/, /**n**/. What is the fourth sound you hear?" [Make sure to emphasize the fourth sound.] If your child gives the correct answer, great. If not, model the correct response: "When I hear the word **drink** [wriggle/point to the fourth finger], I hear the /**n**/ sound. The /**n**/ sound is made by the letter **N,** like in **no**."

Step 7: Move on to the last sound. Stretch the word out, using your fingers as a visual cue: "/**d**/, /**r**/, /ĭ/, /**n**/, /**k**/. What is the last sound you hear in **drink**? [Make sure to emphasize the last sound.]" If your child gives the correct answer, great. If not, model the correct response: "When I hear the word **drink** [wriggle/point to the fifth finger], I hear the /**k**/ sound at the end. The /**k**/ sound is made by the letter **K,** like in **kite**."

Step 8: Now put all five fingers down. Slowly Stretch the word again, putting a finger in the air with each sound, "/**d**/, /**r**/, /**ĭ**/, /**n**/, /**k**/."

Step 9: Next, say, "Drink is spelled **D-R-I-N-K** [wriggle/point to each finger as you spell the word]."

Step 10: Then Catch the word, saying it all together quickly and bringing your five fingers back into a fist "**drink**."

Optional: Finally, use the note cards to show your child the letters that make up the word, and have him/her manipulate the cards to make the new word.

Optional: Use word cards to practice the Stretch & Catch Reading Strategy.

CHAPTER FIVE

BEGINNING AND ENDING DIGRAPHS

AMANDA MCNAMARA LOWE

GREEN TWL WORDS

think	each
water	which
again	read
out	need
ride	hand
day	house
under	mother
there	father
now	still
been	she
soon	their
who	went
when	will
where	about
why	would
may	like
say	time
want	look
well	two
thank	more
that	write
one	number
have	way
here	people
words	ask
because	than
were	called
turn	its
jump	long
run	get
play	made
use	part

DAILY READING

As your child moves through more features, he/she is becoming a good reader. Not only is your child able to figure out unknown words using the Stretch & Catch Reading Strategy, but he/she is becoming more fluent in reading because he/she automatically knows TWL words. Knowing TWL words helps your child become a fluent reader because it prevents him/her from getting stuck on TWL words while reading. Your child is able to read appropriately leveled books on his/her own and harder books with guidance.

It is important that your child continue reading to you daily. As your child reads to you, he/she needs to use the Stretch & Catch Reading Strategy to figure out any short-vowel words, blend words, and digraphs. Encourage your child to also use picture and word clues surrounding the unknown words while reading. If your child has become a more fluent reader, he/she does not have to point to each word while reading anymore.

When children read at their independent level, they get to practice skills such as fluency. As your child continues to memorize the TWL words and learns more Stretch & Catch features, he/she will become a more fluent reader. If your child is still reading slowly word by word and Stretching & Catching almost every word as he/she reads, try finding easier books for him/her. Sometimes, stepping down a level in reading is actually beneficial to a child who is struggling. When a child isn't reading word by word but is reading with more fluency, the child gains more confidence. You can move on to harder books again as your child gains confidence.

STRETCH & CATCH BEGINNING AND ENDING DIGRAPHS

Digraphs are two letters that together make one sound. In this chapter, your child will learn that the number of sounds heard in a word (or fingers put up) won't always coordinate with the number of letters in each word as he/she learned previously.

Digraphs, like blends, can be found at the beginning and end of words. The digraphs and key words we will be discussing are /sh/ as in **ship**, voiced /th/ as in **this**, voiceless /th/ as in **thin**, /wh/ as in **whip**, and /ch/ as in **chin**.

There are two categories for the /th/ sound. That is because /th/ can make either a voiced or voiceless sound and your child needs to learn that both sounds are spelled with the letters **T** and **H**. Both the voiced and voiceless /th/ place the tongue between the teeth, but the voiced /th/ vibrates in the mouth, whereas the voiceless /th/ does not vibrate in the mouth. When you introduce the **th** digraph, you can show your child the two sounds by using the keywords, **this** and **thin** (you will only feel the vibration if you say the word out loud).

After your child has mastered beginning digraphs, he/she will move on to ending digraphs. The ending digraphs you will introduce within this chapter are /sh/ as in **dish**, /ch/ as in **rich**, /th/ as in **math** (the /th/ ending digraph makes only one sound), and /ck/ as in **duck**.

An important note for you, the adult, to remember is that the /ck/ sound at the end of a short-vowel word is always made with **CK**. This is a great trick for you to tell your child when he/she begins to spell long-vowel words that end with the /k/ sound. Long-vowel words ending with the /k/ sound usually end with the letters **KE**. This is not information that your child needs to know now, but it will be beneficial to him/her in Chapters Six and Seven.

In each lesson, you will introduce a new digraph. Each lesson can last one day, one week, or several weeks. It all depends on how long your child requires to master the concept of digraphs. If one new digraph per lesson is too easy, you may introduce two or more digraphs.

Not many words begin with digraphs and contain only short vowels, so you will see that there are not many words to introduce to your child per feature. As you move through higher features, you will encounter more digraphs in words that contain long vowels and R-controlled vowel words.

Remember that after your child has completed the words within each feature, you can use the assessment tool in Chapter One to assess your child. A score of 80% is mastery within each feature, but you may choose to stay in a feature for as long as your child needs. If you feel your child does well during your lessons, however, you can move on to the next feature even if he/she scores lower than an 80% on the assessment. You can decide when your child is ready to move to the next feature.

Please also remember that Stretching & Catching should be done three to five days per week. You can Stretch & Catch each time with one or more words, and you can take as long as your child needs for each lesson.

In addition to Stretching & Catching words, your child needs to continue to use the Stretch & Catch Reading Strategy during his/her daily reading.

This chapter contains an additional activity that can be done before your child is introduced to digraphs. I recommend using this activity to introduce Features 12 and 13.

OPTIONAL TEMPLATE FOR INTRODUCING FEATURES 12–13

*I recommend using note cards to introduce the digraph before each lesson. If you do not have time to do this step, it is okay; you will just explain it during your Stretch & Catch lesson. If you do have time for the introductory note cards, simply write a digraph word from the feature. For example, if you are introducing Feature 12, Lesson 1: /sh/ digraphs, you can use the word **ship**.*

Step 1: Place the digraph word on the table.

Step 2: Say, "Do you notice anything about this word?" Encourage your child to notice the digraph letters at the beginning of the word.

Step 3: Say, "I'm going to Stretch & Catch this word for you."

Step 4: Stretch & Catch the digraph word: "(**Digraph sound**) [first finger up], (**vowel sound**) [second finger up], (**third sound**) [third finger up]."

Step 5: Catch the word (**word**).

Step 6: Say, "Did you notice that the (**digraph letters**) only made one sound? The (**digraph sound**) sound is a digraph. A digraph is when two letters make one new sound."

Step 7: Now have your child Stretch & Catch the same word.

Step 8: Now tell your child that you will be Stretching & Catching more (**digraph sound**) words.

TEMPLATE FEATURE 12
(adult-led Stretch & Catch)

Choose a word.

Step 1: Say, "We are going to spell the word (**word**)."

Step 2: Now tell your child, "When I say the word (**beginning digraph**) [sound the digraph out and lift first finger], (**vowel sound**) [sound the vowel out and lift second finger], (**third sound**) [sound the letter out and lift third finger], do you see that I hear three sounds? But my first sound is (**beginning digraph**) [wriggle/point to first finger]. How many letters make that sound?" Your child should answer **two letters**. [If your child can't answer this correctly, move to the bullet point below to clarify digraphs. If your child is able to answer correctly, move to Step 3.]

- Say, "In the past, when we heard three sounds in a word, there were three letters. Let's listen to the first sound in this word: (**beginning digraph**) [wriggle/point to first finger]. Did you hear the digraph sound?" With all three fingers still up, reinforce the digraph sound by saying the digraph sound in the word again while wriggling/pointing the first finger: "(**Beginning digraph**). The two letters (**digraph letters**) make this sound."

Step 3: Say, "What two letters make the (**digraph sound**) sound? [Wriggle/point to first finger.]" If your child says the correct letters, that is great. If he/she gives an incorrect response, model the correct response: "The (**beginning digraph**) sound is made by the letters (**digraph letters**), like in (**key word**)." (Notice the use of the key word to model the correct response.)

Step 4: Sound out the first two sounds, stopping at the second sound "(**digraph sound**), (**vowel sound**)". With three fingers up, wriggle/point to the second finger. Say, "What letter makes the (**vowel sound**) sound?" If your child gives the correct response, great. If not, model the correct response: "The (**vowel sound**) sound is the letter (**letter**), like in (**key word**)."

Step 5: Still holding three fingers up, stretch the word out, using your fingers as a visual cue: "(**Beginning digraph**) [wriggle/point to first finger], (**vowel sound**) [wriggle/point to second finger], (**third sound**) [wriggle/point to third finger]. What is the last sound you hear in (**word**)?" Make sure to emphasize the last sound "(**third sound**)". If your child gives the correct answer, great. If not, model the correct response: "When I hear the word (**word**) [wriggle/point to the third finger], I hear the (**third sound**) sound at the end. The (**third sound**) sound is the letter (**letter**), like in (**key word**)."

Step 6: Now put all three fingers down. Slowly Stretch the word again: "(**Beginning digraph**) [sound the digraph out and lift first finger], (**vowel sound**) [sound the vowel out and lift second finger], (**third sound**) [sound the letter out and lift third finger]."

Step 7: Next, say, "(**Word**) is spelled (**spelling of word**)," [wriggle/point to each finger as you spell the word, emphasizing the first two letters with only your first finger].

Step 8: Then Catch the word, saying it all together quickly and bringing your three fingers back into a fist (**word**).

Optional: Finally, use the note cards to show your child the letters that make up the word, and have him/her manipulate the cards to make the new word.

Optional: Use word cards to practice the Stretch & Catch Reading Strategy.

TEMPLATE FEATURE 13
(adult-led Stretch & Catch)

Step 1: Say, "We are going to spell the word (**word**)."

Step 2: Now tell your child, "When I say the word (**first sound**) [sound the letter out and lift first finger], (**vowel sound**) [sound the vowel out and lift second finger], (**ending digraph sound**) [sound the digraph out and lift third finger] do you see that I hear three sounds? But my last sound is (**ending digraph**) [wriggle/point to third finger]. How many letters make that sound?" Your child should answer **two letters**. If your child can't answer this correctly, move to the bullet point below to clarify digraphs. If your child is able to answer, move to Step 3.

- Say, "Before, when we heard three sounds in a word, there were three letters. Let's listen to the last sound in this word: (**ending digraph**) [wriggle/point to first finger]. Did you hear the digraph sound?" With all three fingers still up, reinforce the digraph sound by saying the digraph sound in the word again while wriggling/pointing to the third finger. "(**Ending digraph**). The two letters (**digraph letters**) make this sound. When we get to this sound, we will remember that there will be two letters for this one finger [wriggle/point to third finger]."

Step 3: Say: "When I say (**word**), I hear (**first sound**) [wriggle/point to first finger]. What letter is the (**first sound**) sound?" If your child says the correct letter, that is great. If your child gives an incorrect response, model the correct response by saying, "The (**first sound**) sound is made by (**letter**), like in (**key word**)."

Step 4: Sound out the first two sounds, stopping at the second sound. "(**First sound**) (**vowel sound**)." [With three fingers up, wriggle/point to the second finger.] Say, "What letter makes the (**vowel sound**) sound?" If your child gives the correct response, great. If not, model the correct response: "The (**vowel sound**) sound is the letter (**letter**), like in (**key word**)."

Step 5: Still holding three fingers up, stretch the word out, using your fingers as a visual cue, wriggling/pointing to each finger as you say the sound. "(**first sound**), (**vowel sound**), (**ending digraph sound**)." Then say, "What is the digraph sound you hear in (**word**)?" (Make sure to emphasize the digraph sound). If your child gives the correct answer, great. If not, model the correct response: "When I hear the word (**word**) [wriggle/point to third finger], I hear the (**ending digraph sound**) sound at the end. The (**ending digraph sound**) sound has two letters. What two letters make the (**ending digraph sound**) sound?" If your child says the correct letters, that is great. If he/she gives an incorrect response, model the correct response: "The (**ending digraph**) sound is made by the letters (**digraph letters**), like in (**key word**)."

Step 6: Now put all three fingers down. Slowly Stretch the word again, putting a finger in the air with each sound, "(**first sound**), (**vowel sound**), (**ending digraph sound**)."

Step 7: Next, say, "(**Word**) is spelled (**spelling of word**) [wriggle/point to each finger as you spell the word, emphasizing the last two letters with only your third finger]."

Step 8: Then Catch the word, saying it all together quickly and bringing your three fingers back into a fist (**word**).

Optional: Finally, use the note cards to show your child the letters that make up the word, and have him/her manipulate the cards to make the new word.

Optional: Use word cards to practice the Stretch & Catch Reading Strategy.

TEMPLATE FEATURE 12
(child-led Stretch & Catch)

Step 1: Say, "Can you Stretch & Catch the word (**word**)?"

Step 2: Your child will Stretch the word out, putting one finger in the air per sound he/she says.

Step 3: If your child Stretched the word correctly, move to Step 4. If your child Stretched the word incorrectly, move to the bullet point below.

- Say, "When I say (**beginning digraph sound**) [sound the letter out and lift first finger], (**vowel sound**) [sound the letter out and lift second finger], (**third sound**) [sound the letter out and lift third finger], do you see that I hear three sounds? But what two letters make the first sound we hear in (**beginning digraph sound**)?" If your child does not respond with the correct answer, say, "Remember the first sound is a digraph and is made up of two letters." If your child answers with the correct letters, great, move to the next bullet point. If not, again sound each letter out while wriggling/pointing to the finger and saying each letter that corresponds with that sound: "(**Beginning digraph sound and letters**), (**vowel sound and letter**), (**third sound and letter**)."
- Now have your child Stretch this word.

Step 4: Next, your child will look at his/her fingers and spell the word.

Step 5: Now have your child Catch the word, saying it all together quickly and bringing the fingers back into a fist. *Remember this is a technique that your child will need with the reading strategy.*

Optional: Finally, use the note cards to show your child the letters that make up the word, and have him/her manipulate the cards to make the new word.

Optional: Use word cards to practice the Stretch & Catch Reading Strategy.

TEMPLATE FEATURE 13
(child-led Stretch & Catch)

Step 1: Say, "Can you Stretch & Catch the word (**word**)?"

Step 2: Your child will Stretch the word out, putting one finger in the air per sound he/she says.

Step 3: If your child Stretched the word correctly, move to Step 4. If your child Stretched the word incorrectly, move to the bullet point below.

- Say, "When I say (**first sound**) [sound the letter out and lift first finger], (**vowel sound**) [sound the letter out and lift second finger], (**ending digraph sound**) [sound the letter out and lift the third finger], do you see that I hear three sounds? But what two letters make the last sound we hear (**ending digraph sound**)?" If your child does not respond with the correct answer, say, "Remember the last sound is a digraph and is made up of two letters." If your child answers with the correct letters, great, move to the next bullet point. If not, again sound each letter out while wriggling/pointing to the finger and saying each letter that corresponds with that sound: "(**First sound** and **letter**), (**vowel sound** and **letter**), (**ending digraph sound** and **letters**)."
- Now have your child Stretch the word out.

Step 4: Next, your child will look at his/her fingers and spell the word.

Step 5: Now have your child Catch the word, saying it all together quickly and bringing the fingers back into a fist. *Remember, this is a technique that your child will need with the reading strategy.*

Optional: Finally, use the note cards to show your child the letters that make up the word, and have him/her manipulate the cards to make the new word.

Optional: Use word cards to practice the Stretch & Catch Reading Strategy.

LESSONS FOR FEATURES 12–13

FEATURE 12 WORDS

12:1: **/sh/**: ship, sham, shop, shut, shot, shelf
12-2: **voiced /th/**: this, them, than, that, then, thus
12-2: **voiceless /th/**: thin, think, thud, thank
12-3: **/wh/**: whim, whip, whisk, whiz, when, which
12-4: **/ch/**: chant, chat, champ, chest, chin, chip, chop

FEATURE 13 WORDS

13-1: **/sh/**: flash, crash, gush, brush, blush, wish, trash, slush, rash, cash, fish, flush, dash, smash, bash
13-2: **/ch/**: rich, inch, much, such, which
13-3: **/th/**: bath, math, path, moth, cloth
13-4: **/ck/**: duck, stuck, check, sock, clock, stick, stack, Jack, kick

EXAMPLE EXERCISE FEATURE 12
(adult-led)

ship

Step 1: Say, "We are going to spell the word **ship**."

Step 2: Tell your child, "When I say the word /**sh**/ [lift first finger], /**ĭ**/ [lift second finger], /**p**/ [lift third finger], do you see that I hear three sounds? But my first sound is /**sh**/ [wriggle/point to first finger]. How many letters make that sound?" Your child should answer that two letters make the /**sh**/ sound. If your child can't answer this correctly, move to the bullet point to clarify digraphs. If your child answers correctly, move to Step 3.

> • Say, "Before, when we heard three sounds in a word, there were three letters. Let's listen to the first sound in this word: /**sh**/ [wriggle/point to first finger]. Did you hear the digraph sound?" With all three fingers still up, reinforce the digraph sound by saying the digraph sound in the word again while wriggling/pointing to the first finger]: "/**sh**/. The two letters **S** and **H** make this sound."

Step 3: Say, "What two letters make the /**sh**/ sound [wriggle/point to first finger]?" If your child says the correct letters, that is great. If he/she gives an incorrect response, model the correct response: "The /**sh**/ sound is made by the letters **S** and **H**, like in **ship**." (Notice the use of the key word to model the correct response.)

Step 4: Sound out the first two sounds, stopping at the second sound, "/**sh**/ /**ĭ**/". With three fingers up, wriggle/point to the second finger. Say, "What letter makes the /**ĭ**/ sound?" If your child gives the correct response, great. If not, model the correct response: "The /**ĭ**/ sound is the letter **I**, like in **itch**."

Step 5: Still holding three fingers up, stretch the word out, using your fingers as a visual cue, "/**sh**/ /**ĭ**/ /**p**/." Then say, "What is the last sound you hear in **ship**?" Make sure to emphasize the last sound "/**p**/." If your child gives the correct answer, great. If not, model the correct response: "When I hear the word **ship** [wriggle/point to third finger], I hear the /**p**/ sound at the end. The /**p**/ sound is made by the letter **P**, like in **popsicle**."

Step 6: Now put all three fingers down. Slowly Stretch the word again, putting a finger in the air with each sound, "/**sh**/ /**ĭ**/ /**p**/."

Step 7: Next, say, "**Ship** is spelled **S-H-I-P** [wriggle/point to each finger as you spell the word, emphasizing the first two letters using only your first finger]."

Step 8: Then Catch the word, saying it all together quickly and bringing your three fingers back into a fist "**ship**."

Optional: Finally, use the note cards to show your child the letters that make up the word, and have him/her manipulate the cards to make the new word.

Optional: Use word cards to practice the Stretch & Catch Reading Strategy.

EXAMPLE EXERCISE FEATURE 13
(adult-led)

Step 1: Say, "We are going to spell the word **rich**."

Step 2: Tell your child, "When I say the word /**r**/ [lift first finger], /ĭ/ [lift second finger], /**ch**/ [lift third finger], do you see that I hear three sounds? But my last sound is /**ch**/ [wriggle/point to third finger]. How many letters make that sound?" Your child should answer that two letters make that sound. If your child can't answer this correctly, move to the bullet point below to clarify digraphs. If your child is able to answer, move to Step 3.

- Say, "Before, when we heard three sounds in a word, there were three letters. Let's listen to the last sound in this word: /**ch**/ [wriggle/point to third finger]. Did you hear the digraph sound?" With all three fingers still up, reinforce the digraph sound by saying the digraph sound in the word again while wriggling/pointing the third finger: "/**ch**/. Two letters makes this sound. So when we get to this sound, we will remember that there will be the two letters **C** and **H** for this one finger [wriggle/point to third finger]."

Step 3: Say: "When I say **rich,** I hear /**r**/ [wriggle/point to first finger]. What letter is the /**r**/ sound?" If your child says the letter **R**, that is great. If your child gives an incorrect response, model the correct response by saying, "The /**r**/ sound is the letter **R**, like in **run**."

Step 4: Sound out the first two sounds, stopping at the second sound, "/**r**/ /ĭ/." With three fingers up, wriggle/point to the second finger, and say, "What letter makes the /ĭ/ sound?" If your child gives the correct response, great. If not, model the correct response: "The /ĭ/ sound is the letter **I**, like in **itch**."

Step 5: Still holding three fingers up, Stretch the word out, using your fingers as a visual cue, wriggling/pointing to each finger as you say the sound: "/**r**/ /ĭ/ /**ch**/. What is the digraph sound you hear in **rich**?" Make sure to emphasize the last sound "/**ch**/." If your child gives the correct answer, great. If not, model the correct response: "When I hear the word **rich** [wriggle/point to third finger], I hear the /**ch**/ sound at the end. The /**ch**/ sound has two letters. What two letters make the /**ch**/ sound?" If your child says the correct letters, that is great. If the child gives an incorrect response, model the correct response: "The /**ch**/ sound is made by the letters **C** and **H**, like in **rich**." (Notice the use of the key word to model the correct response.)

Step 6: Now put all three fingers down. Slowly Stretch the word again putting a finger in the air with each sound, "/**r**/ /ĭ/ /**ch**/."

Step 7: Next, say, "**Rich** is spelled **R-I-C-H** [wriggle/point to each finger as you spell the word, emphasizing the last two letters using only your third finger]."

Step 8: Then Catch the word, saying it all together quickly and bringing your three fingers back into a fist "**RICH**."

Optional: Finally, use the note cards to show your child the letters that make up the word, and have him/her manipulate the cards to make the new word.

Optional: Use word cards to practice the Stretch & Catch Reading Strategy.

THE LAST PHASE OF STRETCH & CATCH

CHAPTER SIX

LONG VOWELS WITH A SILENT E

AMANDA MCNAMARA LOWE

RED TWL WORDS

give	three
take	four
good	five
only	six
new	seven
most	eight
very	nine
after	ten
just	zero
name	does
great	another
through	large
much	must
before	try
right	kind
too	change
tell	found
boy	answer
such	world
even	red
follow	orange
want	blue
show	yellow
also	green
around	purple
one	black
two	brown

DAILY READING

Children begin to read silently as they learn the features of long vowels. During this feature, your child will probably begin to read easy chapter books. It is important that you listen to your child read the first five sentences of any book, to make sure it is a "just right" book for your child. Remind your child to use the five-finger test from Chapter One to find a "just right" book.

Continue having your child use the Stretch & Catch Reading Strategy to figure out any unknown words. Encourage your child to also use word clues surrounding the unknown word while reading. As your child progresses through this chapter, you will begin to notice that he/she can Stretch & Catch silently. Encourage your child to do this while reading.

In this chapter, your child will continue to see that the number of letters in a word doesn't always correspond with the number of sounds that a word produces, which in turn helps him/her become more advanced as a reader and speller. Similar to Stretching digraphs, Stretching and Catching long vowels will force your child's brain to look at a word's pattern before Stretching & Catching.

STRETCH & CATCH LONG VOWELS WITH a SILENT E

A long vowel says its own name. The diacritical mark for a long vowel is called a macron. It's a straight line over the vowel. For example, in the word **cāke**, the macron is over the **A** to show that it's a long vowel. When we begin to teach long vowels, we first talk only about the **vowel/consonant/e** words, also referred to as the **silent e** and **magic e**. In this book, we will refer to it as the **silent e**. The **silent e** at the end of the word helps that vowel talk and say its name.

This will be the first chapter in which you introduce vowel patterns to your child. These vowel patterns are the rules we use for spelling words that contain long vowels. Your child must also understand that there are always exceptions to these rules. I have tried to place many exceptions in the TWL lists. Make sure to point out these exceptions to your child while he or she is learning. For example, your child will learn the long-a (**ā**) vowel pattern **āCe** (**ā/consonant/silent e**). I will explain that this **A** is long if the letter **A** is followed by a **consonant** and then an **E**. An exception to this rule is the word **have**. Your child needs to be able to identify the word **have** and to understand that this word doesn't follow the rule and therefore can't be sounded out. When you Stretch & Catch a long vowel, it doesn't make more sounds than the short-vowel word does, so it is important that your child understand the concept that **kite** is a long-vowel word because the pattern is **vCe** (**vowel/consonant/silent e**) and not pronounced like the word **kit**, which has a **cVc** (**consonant/vowel/consonant**) pattern. (I use **cVc** to refer to the short-vowel pattern. Your child does not need to learn about the **cVc** pattern but will have to learn the **vCe pattern**.) In layman's terms, the short-vowel word has no **silent e** to make it a long-vowel word.

At this point in Stretch & Catch, your child will not need to use the **key words**, because he/she knows his/her sounds. If your child identifies an incorrect letter for any sound, you will simply tell him/her the correct letter that corresponds with the sound.

In each lesson, you will introduce a new long vowel. Each lesson will last more than one day, and can last up to a week or a month. Move on to the next feature only once your child has mastered the concept of each long vowel with a **silent e**. (We will not be covering **ē** in this chapter because very few words have a pattern of **ē/consonant/silent e**. It will be discussed in Chapter Eight, Feature 19.)

Below, you will find the patterns within words that your child needs to recognize when using the Stretch & Catch Reading Strategy for sounding out and/or spelling unknown words. It is helpful to teach your child the actual word pattern. For example, when you teach your child about **ā** words, show him/her how the word uses an **āCe** pattern. If you prefer to simply teach the pattern of the **silent e**, that is fine, but your child will have an easier time with future features if he/she begins using the name for each pattern now.

LONG-VOWEL PATTERNS
vCe = vowel/consonant/silent e

- **Long-A (ā) pattern: āCe**
  ○ cake = **a**/consonant (**k**)/**silent e**
  ○ tape = **a**/consonant (**p**)/**silent e**

- **Long-I (ī) pattern: īCe**
  ○ mice = **i**/consonant (**c**)/**silent e**
  ○ bike = **i**/consonant (**k**)/**silent e**

- **Long-O (ō) pattern: ōCe**
  ○ rode = **o**/consonant (**d**)/**silent e**
  ○ note = **o**/consonant (**t**)/**silent e**

- **Long-U (ū) pattern: ūCe**
  (Long U makes its own name, /ū/, when long but can also make the /oo/ sound when long.)
  ○ plume = **u**/consonant (**m**)/**silent e**
  ○ cute = **u**/consonant (**t**)/**silent e**

Remember, after your child has completed the words within each feature, you can use the assessment tool in Chapter One to determine if he/she can move on to the next feature. A score of 80% is mastery within each feature. You may choose to stay in a feature for as long as your child needs. Remember, you can move on to the next feature if your child scored lower than 80% if he/she has done well during lessons. You can decide when your child is ready to move to the next feature.

OPTIONAL TEMPLATE FOR INTRODUCING FEATURES 14–17

*I recommend using note cards to introduce the long vowel before each lesson. If you do not have time to do this step, it is okay; you will just explain it during your Stretch & Catch lesson. If you do have time for the introductory note cards, simply create one with a long-vowel word from the feature your child is being introduced to, and another note card with a short-vowel word that has the same vowel as the long-vowel word. For example, if you are introducing Feature 14, Lesson 1: āCe words, you can use the words **tape** and **tap**. The words do not have to be so similar, but at first, it's sometimes helpful to use words that are so similar if your child can't hear the difference between long and short vowels or to help show how a **silent e** at the end of a word makes the word a long vowel word. You could also use the words **tape** and **cat** to introduce this lesson; the important part is that the vowel is the same. You will find the words for this activity in the appendix.*

Step 1: Place the short-vowel note card on the table in front of your child.

Step 2: Ask your child to Stretch the word.

Step 3: Then have your child Catch the word quickly.

Step 4: Now say, "Do you hear the short vowel in this word? The letter (**short-vowel letter**) says (**short-vowel sound**), so it is a short vowel. Now I'm going to show you a new word."

Step 5: Place the long-vowel word next to the short-vowel word.

Step 6: Say, "What is the difference between the two note cards?" Encourage your child to notice the **E** at the end of the long-vowel word.

Step 7: Say, "I'm going to Stretch & Catch this word for you."

Step 8: Stretch & Catch the long-vowel word: "(**First sound**) [first finger up], (**long-vowel sound**) [second finger up], (**third sound**) [third finger up]."

Step 9: Say, "Notice that this word has the same number of sounds as the word (**short-vowel word**). What is the difference between the words (**short-vowel word**) and (**long-vowel word**)?" If your child hears that the short-vowel word says (**short-vowel sound**) and the long-vowel word says (**long-vowel sound**) great; move to Step 10. If not, move to the bullet point below.

- Say, "Do you hear that when I say (**short-vowel word**), the (**vowel letter**) says (**short-vowel sound**)?"
- Say, "Do you hear that when I say (**long-vowel word**), the (**vowel letter**) says (**long-vowel sound**)? When a vowel says its name, like (**long-vowel sound**) in (**long-vowel word**), it is called a long vowel. Why do you think (**long-vowel word**) says a long sound and (**short-vowel word**) says a short sound?" You want the child to see that the **E** at the end of the long-vowel word changes the vowel sound. If the child sees the **E** makes the vowel long, move to Step 10. If not, move to the bullet point below.
- If your child doesn't notice the **E** at the end of the long-vowel word, say, "Notice there is an **E** at the end of the word (**long-vowel word**). We call that a **silent e**. The **silent e** at the end of the word helps that vowel talk and say its name. When a vowel says its own name, it is a long vowel, but when you Stretch & Catch a long vowel, it doesn't make more sounds than the short vowel does."

Step 10: Say, "What is the pattern in the word (**long-vowel word**)? You want your child to recognize the pattern (**vowel pattern**) makes the vowel long. If your child identifies the pattern correctly, great; move to Step 11. Otherwise move to the bullet point below.

- Tell your child, "When you see the pattern **vCe** in a word, the **E** makes the vowel a long-vowel word, like in (**long-vowel word**) [have your child point to the pattern on the notecard]."

Step 11: Now have your child Stretch & Catch the same word.

Step 12: Next, tell your child that he/she will be Stretching & Catching more long-vowel words with **silent e** endings.

TEMPLATE FEATURES 14–17
(adult-led Stretch & Catch)

Step 1: Say, "We are going to spell the word (**word**)."

Step 2: Tell your child, "When I say the word (**first sound**) [sound the letter out and lift first finger], (**long-vowel sound**) [sound the vowel out and lift second finger], (**third sound**) [sound the letter out and lift third finger], do you see that I hear three sounds? I hear three sounds, but how many letters does my word have?" If your child can tell you there are four letters because this is a **long-vowel word**, move to Step 3. If your child does not realize the word has a long-vowel sound, move to the bullet point below to clarify the **vCe** pattern.

- Say, "My vowel sound is (**long-vowel sound**) [wriggle/point to second finger]. How many letters make that sound?" If your child doesn't say that it uses two letters (**vowel letter** and **silent e**), continue; if he/she gives the correct response, move on to Step 3.
- Say, "When a vowel says its name, it is a long vowel. When I say the word (**first sound**) [lift first finger], (**long-vowel sound**) [lift second finger], (**third sound**) [lift third finger], do you hear the vowel saying its own name? Now, what pattern in this word (**word**) says the long vowel?" At this point, your child should answer **vCe** or say the vowel is long because there is a **silent e** at the end of the word. If your child does not know the answer, remind him/her by saying, "Long vowels are made with the pattern **vCe**. That means there is a **silent e** at the end of this word. So when we get to the end of this word, we will have to remember to add a **silent e** when we Stretch & Catch."

Step 3: Say, "When I say (**word**), I hear (**first sound**) [wriggle/point to first finger]. What letter makes the (**first sound**) sound?" If your child says the correct letter, that is great. If your child gives an incorrect response, model the correct response by saying, "The (**first sound**) sound is made by the letter (**letter**)."

Step 4: Sound out the first two sounds, stopping at the second sound. "(**First sound**) (**long-vowel sound**)" [with three fingers up, wriggle/point to the second finger]. Say, "What letter makes the (**long-vowel sound**) sound?" If your child gives the correct response, great. If not, model the correct response: "The (**long-vowel sound**) sound is made by the letter (**letter**)."

Step 5: Still holding three fingers up, Stretch the word out, "(**first sound**) (**long-vowel sound**) (**third sound**)" [wriggling/pointing to each finger as you say the sound]. Say, "What is the last sound you hear in (**word**)?" (Make sure to emphasize the last sound.) If your child gives the correct answer, great. If not, model the correct response: "The (**third sound**) sound is made by the letter (**letter**)."

Step 6: With three fingers still up, wriggle/point to the second finger to emphasize the long-vowel sound, and ask, "Now what do we need to add to the end of this word to make the (**long-vowel sound**) sound?" If your child gives the correct answer (**silent e**), great. If not, model the correct response: "Remember, the long vowel needs help to say its name. What pattern makes (**word**) a long-vowel word?" If your child doesn't reply that it's **vCe** or **silent e**, tell him/her.

Step 7: Now put all three fingers down. Slowly Stretch the word again, "(**first sound**) (**long-vowel sound**) (**third sound**)" [putting a finger in the air with each sound].

Step 8: Next, say, "(**Word** is spelled (**spelling of word**)." [Wriggle/point to each finger as you spell the word, emphasizing the last two letters using only your third finger].

Step 9: Then Catch the word, saying it all together quickly and bringing your three fingers back into a fist (**word**).

Optional: Finally, use the note cards to show your child the letters that make up the word, and have him/her manipulate the cards to make the new word.

Optional: Use word cards to practice the Stretch & Catch Reading Strategy.

TEMPLATE FEATURES 14–17
(child-led Stretch & Catch)

Step 1: Say, "Can you Stretch & Catch the word (**word**)?"

Step 2: Your child will Stretch the word out, putting one finger in the air per sound he/she says.

Step 3: Next, your child will look at his/her fingers and spell the word.

Step 4: If your child spelled the long-vowel word correctly, move to Step 5. If your child forgot to add the **silent e**, move to the bullet point below.

- Say, "What is the vowel sound you hear in the word (**word**)?" If your child doesn't say the long-vowel sound, tell him/her the answer.
- Say, "When a vowel says its name, it is a long vowel. When I say the word (**first sound**) [lift first finger], (**long-vowel sound**) [lift second finger], (**third sound**) [lift third finger], do you hear the vowel saying its own name? How many letters make that sound? What pattern does the word (**word**) follow to say the long vowel instead of the short vowel?" At this point, your child should answer that the word uses the **vCe** pattern or say that the vowel is long because there is a **silent e** at the end of the word. If your child does not know the answer, remind him/her by saying, "Long vowels are made with the pattern **vCe**. That means there is a **silent e** at the end of this word. You will have to remember to add a **silent e** when you Stretch & Catch."
- Now have your child Stretch and spell the word again.

Step 5: Now have your child Catch the word by saying it all together quickly and bringing the fingers back into a fist. *Remember, this is a technique that your child will need with the reading strategy.*

Optional: Finally, use the note cards to show your child the letters that make up the word, and have him/her manipulate the cards to make the new word.

Optional: Use word cards to practice the Stretch & Catch Reading Strategy.

LESSONS FOR FEATURES 14–17

FEATURE 14 WORDS

14-1: **Long-A (ā) pattern āCe**: lake, bake, cake, take, flake, plate, face, whale, place, grape, gate, face, late, state, male, tape, hate, cane, fade, mate, plane

FEATURE 15 WORDS

15-1: **Long-I (ī) pattern īCe**: dice, fine, hike, lime, mile, nine, wipe, size, ride, line, mine, side, time, wife, five, bite, kite, site, lite, dime, ride, time, pine, ripe, spite

FEATURE 16 WORDS

16-1: **Long-O (ō) pattern ōCe**: bone, hole, woke, nose, pole, broke, vote, choke, stone, wrote, drove, close, those, clone, zone, note, code, tone, robe, hope

FEATURE 17 WORDS

17-1: **Long-U (ū) pattern ūCe** (*Long U can say its name, as in **use**, but it can also say /oo/, as in **duke**.*): use, mute, June, duke, fume, muse, dune, lute, tune, rude, mule, dude, brute, flute, tube, dude, plume, cute, use, huge, cube

EXAMPLE EXERCISE FEATURES 14–17
(adult-led)

Step 1: Say, "We are going to spell the word **lake**."

Step 2: Tell your child, "When I say the word /l/ [lift first finger], /ā/ [lift second finger], /k/ [lift third finger], do you see that I hear three sounds? I hear three sounds, but how many letters does my word have?" If your child can tell you there are four letters because this is a long-**A** word with a **silent e** at the end; move to Step 3. If your child does not realize the word has a long-vowel sound made with the **silent e** vowel pattern, move to the bullet point below to clarify the **āCe** pattern.

- Say, "My vowel sound is /ā/ [wriggle/point to second finger]. How many letters make that sound?" If your child doesn't say it takes two letters (**A** and **silent e**), continue with the bullet point below; if he/she gives the correct response, move on to Step 3.
- Say, "When a vowel says its name, it is a long vowel. When I say the word /l/ [lift first finger], /ā/ [lift second finger], /k/ [lift third finger], do you hear the vowel saying its own name? Now, what vowel pattern is in this word, **lake**?" At this point, your child should answer **āCe** or **vCe** or say the vowel is long because there is a **silent e** at the end of the word. If your child does not know the answer, remind him/her by saying, "Long vowels are made with the pattern **vCe**. That means there is a **silent e** at the end of this word. So when we get to the end of this word, we will have to remember to add a **silent e** when we Stretch & Catch."

Step 3: Say, "When I say **lake**, I hear /l/ [wriggle/point to first finger, all three fingers are still up]. What letter makes the /l/ sound?" If your child says the letter **L**, that is great. If your child gives an incorrect response, model by saying, "The /l/ sound is the letter **L**."

Step 4: Sound out the first two sounds, stopping at the second sound, "/l/ /ā/" [wriggling/pointing to the second finger]. Say, "What letter makes the /ā/ sound?" If your child gives the correct response, great. If not, model the correct response: "The /ā/ sound is made by the letter **A**."

Step 5: Still holding three fingers up, Stretch the word out, using your fingers as a visual cue, wriggling/pointing to each finger as you say the sound: "/l/ /ā/ /k/. What is the last sound you hear in **lake**?" (Make sure to emphasize the last sound.) If your child gives the correct answer, great. If not, model the correct response: "The /k/ sound is made by the letter **K**."

Step 6: With three fingers still up, wriggle/point to the second finger to emphasize the long vowel sound, and ask, "Now what do we need to add to the end of this word to make the /ā/ sound?" If your child gives the correct answer (**silent e**), great. If not, model the correct response: "Remember, the long vowel needs help to say its name. What pattern makes this word, **lake,** a long-vowel word?" If your child doesn't reply **āCe**, **vCe**, or **silent e**, tell him/her.

Step 7: Put all three fingers down. Slowly Stretch the word again, "/l/ /ā/ /k/" [putting a finger in the air with each sound].

Step 8: Next, say, "**Lake** is spelled **L-A-K-E** [wriggle or point to each finger as you spell the word, emphasizing the last two letters using only your third finger]."

Step 9: Then Catch the word, saying it all together quickly and bringing your three fingers back into a fist "**lake**".

Optional: Finally, use the note cards to show your child the letters that make up the word, and have him/her manipulate the cards to make the new word.

Optional: Use word cards to practice the Stretch & Catch Reading Strategy.

CHAPTER SEVEN

OTHER COMMON LONG VOWELS

PURPLE TWL WORDS

high	swear
every	important
laugh	children
push	enough
bush	between
truth	idea
front	might
been	something
prince	night
since	watch
ridge	really
buy	almost
guy	school
friend	example
fierce	beginning
weird	sometimes
blood	always
poor	once
build	young
built	together
guide	second
cruel	third
fuel	fourth
flour	fifth
hour	sixth
scour	seventh
sour	eighth
bear	ninth
heart	tenth
wear	without
pear	

DAILY READING

As your child begins to master the difference between short-vowel words and long-vowel words, he/she also begins to read higher-level texts that include long-vowel words with different vowel patterns. Learning these different vowel patterns will allow your child to Stretch & Catch unknown long-vowel words using the Stretch & Catch Reading Strategy. There are very few pictures or drawings in higher-level books, so your child must rely heavily on Stretch & Catch Reading Strategy and context clues to identify unknown words while reading. Continue having your child practice the Stretch & Catch Reading Strategy with note cards or while reading aloud to you.

As this and the following chapters move into more complex decoding skills, your child will become a more advanced reader. Your child will also increase his/her fluency as he/she finishes memorizing the last of the TWL words. The more your child reads, the better a reader he/she will become.

STRETCH & CATCH OTHER COMMON LONG VOWELS

This will be the first chapter in which I give you only the child-led Stretch & Catch templates. At this point in Stretch & Catch, your child has already learned how to Stretch & Catch many features and uses Stretch & Catch as his/her main strategy for sounding out unknown words while reading. Therefore, your child should be able to Stretch & Catch on his/her own with less help. In each child-led Stretch & Catch, I will still provide a bullet point to help clarify any new patterns that your child may need additional support with, as I have in previous chapters.

In the previous chapter, your child was introduced to long vowels with words that follow the **vCe** (**vowel/consonant/silent e**) pattern and we discussed how long vowels say their own name. This chapter consists of other common long-vowel word patterns. In this chapter, we will look at the many other patterns that can make a vowel long. This is important because you want your child to look at an entire word and find the pattern within that word. The more patterns your child is able to identify within words, the more information his/her brain has to analyze any unknown word, find the pattern within that word, and then recognize the unknown word.

FEATURE RULES FOR EACH SPELLING PATTERN

Each feature in this chapter consists of two or more spelling patterns that you will introduce to your child. In order for your child to begin to understand each spelling pattern, you will need to teach each spelling rule when introducing each feature. Within each feature, I suggest which spelling patterns should be taught together, but if you prefer to teach each spelling pattern by itself, you can do that as well.

We will discuss the following spelling patterns and rules for each long vowel. There are always exceptions to every spelling rule within the English language, but I give you these rules because they work most of the time when dissecting unknown words.

FEATURE 18 RULES: long-A (ā) patterns ai, ay (Teach both patterns together.)

- *Spelling rule for ay:* When a word contains an **A** followed by a **Y**, the **Y** becomes a vowel and makes the **A** a long vowel. Notice this pattern is at the end of a long-**A** word and has no consonants that follow. Example: *stay.*

- *Spelling rule for ai:* When a word contains two vowels next to each other, the first vowel (**A**) says its name and the second vowel (**I**) is silent. The silent **I** makes the **A** say its name. You can use this phrase to help your child: "When two vowels are together, the first does the talking the second does the walking." The **ai** spelling pattern is always in the middle of a word and is followed by a consonant. Example: *pain.*

  *Help your child recognize that the **ay** combination is typically at the end of a word, whereas **ai** is typically in the middle of a word. This clue will help your child know when to use the **ay** and when to use the **ai** when spelling long-A words.*

FEATURE 19 RULES: long-E (ē) patterns ē: ee, ea, e (Teach all patterns together.)

- *Spelling rule for ee and ea:* When a word contains two vowels next to each other, the first vowel (**E**) says its name and the second vowel is silent. The patterns **ee** and **ea** are usually found within the middle of a word. There is no rule for when you use **ee** instead of **ea**. Your child will need to memorize which words use which pattern. The more your child sees each word while reading, and the more he/she Stretches & Catches each word, the more likely his/her brain will memorize which pattern is used for each word. Examples: *jeep, reach.*
- *Spelling rule for e:* When a word is one syllable and follows the pattern **Cv (consonant/vowel)**— **Ce (consonant/E)** in this case—the **E** in the word says its name. Example: *he.*

FEATURE 20 RULES: long-I (ī) patterns y, ye, igh, iCC (Teach **y** and **ye** together. Teach **igh** and **iCC** together.)

- *The spelling rule for y and ye:* One-syllable words that end in **Y** usually have the long-**I** sound. Some one-syllable words end with **ye** to make the long-**I** sound. Your child will have to memorize which words end with **y** and which end with **ye**. Again, the more your child sees words with this pattern within reading, and the more your child Stretches & Catches words with this pattern, the more likely his/her brain will memorize the correct pattern within each word. Examples: *my, bye.*
- *Spelling rule for iCC (i/consonant/consonant):* When the letter **I** is followed by two consonants (**iCC**), it makes the long-I sound. Example: *kind.*
- *Spelling rule for igh:* The **igh** pattern also follows the **iCC** rule, but because so many words are spelled with **igh,** this book separates them into two rules. Example, *night.*

FEATURE 21 RULES: long-O (ō) patterns oCC, oa, ow (Teach all patterns together.)

- *Spelling rule for oCC (o/consonant/consonant):* When the letter **O** is followed by two consonants (**oCC**), it makes the long-**O** sound. Example, *cold.*
- *Spelling rule for oa:* When a word contains two vowels next to each other, the first vowel (**O**) says its name and the second vowel (**A**) is silent. The pattern **oa** is usually found within the middle of a word. Example: *coast.*
- *Spelling rule for ow:* When the letter **O** is followed by the letter **W,** the **W** becomes silent and makes the letter **O** say its name. Sometimes **ow** makes the long-**O** sound, as in the word *low,* although many times, the **ow** creates a diphthong (Feature 23), as in *cow.*

FEATURE 22 RULES: long-U (ū) patterns ue, ui, oo, ew (Teach **ue** and **ui** together. Teach **oo** and **ew** together.)

*Remember from the previous chapter that the long U can say its name, as in **June**, and can also say /**oo**/, as in **moon**.*

- *Spelling rule for **ue**:* When a word contains two vowels next to each other, the first vowel (**U**) says its name (or /**oo**/ sound) and the second vowel (**E**) is silent. The **ue** combination is typically at the end of a word. Example: *blue*.
- *Spelling rule for **ui**:* When a word contains two vowels next to each other, the first vowel (**U**) says /**oo**/ and the second vowel (**I**) is silent. The pattern **ui** is typically in the middle of a word. Example: *fruit*.

  *Help your child recognize that the **ue** combination is typically at the end of a word, whereas **ui** is typically in the middle of a word. This clue will help your child know when to use **ue** and when to use **ui** when spelling long-U words.*
- *Spelling rule for **oo**:* When **oo** is next to each other in a word, it can make the long **U** sound /**oo**/. Example: *soon*.
- *Spelling rule **ew**:* When **ew** is next to each other in a word, it makes the long **U** sound /**oo**/. Example: blew.

The more your child Stretches & Catches other long-vowel patterns, the more your child has a chance to memorize the correct spelling for each long-vowel word.

Remember that after your child has completed the spelling patterns within each feature, you can use the assessment tool in Chapter One to determine if he/she can move on to the next feature. Remember also that a score of 80% is mastery within each feature, but you may choose to stay in a feature for as long as your child needs. You can move on to the next feature even if he/she scored lower than 80% if you feel your child does well during your lessons. You can decide when your child is ready to move to the next feature.

OPTIONAL TEMPLATE FOR INTRODUCING FEATURES 18–22

*I recommend using note cards to introduce each feature. If you do not have time to do this step, it is okay; you will just explain it during your Stretch & Catch lesson. If you do have time for the introductory note cards, simply make a note card with a long-vowel word from the feature that your child is being introduced to. For example, if you are introducing Feature 18, Lesson 1 (18-1): long **ai** words, you can use the word **rain.***

Step 1: Place the long-vowel word card on the table.

Step 2: Say, "Do you notice anything about this word?" Encourage your child to notice the particular spelling pattern in the word. *If your child has already been introduced to other common long vowels, he/she might notice a pattern similar to a previous feature pattern, such as, two vowels next to each other.*

Step 3: Say, "I'm going to Stretch & Catch this word for you."

Step 4: Stretch & Catch the word: "(**First sound**) [first finger up], (**long-vowel sound**) [second finger up], (**ending sound**) [third finger up]."

Step 5: Now Catch the word, bringing your fingers together into a fist as you say the word quickly (**word**).

Step 6: Say, "Did you notice that the (**spelling pattern**) made only one sound?" Explain the spelling rule for this spelling pattern.

Step 7: Now have your child Stretch & Catch the same word.

Step 8: Finally, tell your child that he/she will be Stretching & Catching more words using this spelling pattern.

TEMPLATE FEATURES 18–22
(child-led Stretch & Catch)

Step 1: Say, "Can you Stretch & Catch the word (**word**)?"

Step 2: Your child will Stretch the word out, putting one finger in the air per sound he/she says. (Remember he/she should lift only one finger per long-vowel sound even though there may be more letters per sound.)

Step 3: Next, your child will look at his/her fingers and spell the word.

Step 4: If your child spelled the long-vowel word correctly, move to the Step 5. If your child was unable to spell the word correctly, move to the bullet point below for clarification.

- Say, "What is the long-vowel sound you hear in the word (**word**)?" If your child identifies the correct sound move to the next bullet point. Otherwise, continue with this bullet point. If your child doesn't say the correct long-vowel sound, say "I hear the long (**long-vowel sound**) sound in the word (**word**)."
- Say, "What spelling pattern does the word (**word**) follow?" If your child identifies the correct spelling pattern, have him/her Stretch and spell the word again using the spelling pattern and then move to Step 5. If your child is unable to identify the spelling pattern move to the bullet point below.
- Stretch & Catch the word for your child: "When I hear the word (**word**), I hear (**first sound**), [lift first finger], (**second sound**) [lift second finger], (**third sound**) [lift third finger]. The word (**word**) has the (**spelling pattern**) spelling pattern." Now look at your fingers and wriggle/point to each finger as you spell the word correctly for your child: "(**Word**) is spelled (**spelling of word**)." (Keep in mind that some fingers will represent two or more letters.)
- Now have your child Stretch and spell the same word. Move to Step 5.

Step 5: Now have your child Catch the word, saying it all together quickly and bringing his/her fingers back into a fist.

Optional: Finally, use the note cards to show your child the letters that make up the word, and have him/her manipulate the cards to make the new word. *This is a very helpful activity if your child is having trouble with the spelling pattern.*

Optional: Use word cards to practice the Stretch & Catch Reading Strategy.

LESSONS FOR FEATURES 18–22

FEATURE 18
Long-A (ā) Words
18-1: **ai:** paint, rain, tail, mail, sail, pain, vain, gain, claim, waist, wait, maid, aim, grain, brain, braid, bait, aid, rail, pail, nail, main, train, tail, wait, paid, jail, chain, faint, plain, stain, raid, hail, drain, snail, praise, slain, Spain, afraid, frail

18-2: **ay:** stay, day, lay, jay, may, play, say, stay, way, clay, hay, pay, ray, away, display, gray, pray, tray, slay

FEATURE 19
Long-E (ē) Words
19-1: **ee:** seed, feed, beep, bee, feet, see, seen, seem, week, beef, deep, meet, green, need, sheep, sleep, free, knee, queen, sheet, street, teeth, wheel, bleed, cheek, creek, creep, greed, greet, heel, peel, speech, speed, steep, sweep, sweet, deed, eel, kneel, preen, reef, sleek, breed, flee, keen, seep

19-2: **ea:** beat, meat, squeal, bean, clean, each, eat, leave, mean, real, sea, seat, teach, beach, east, meat, pea, reach, read, scream, sneak, bean, beast, cream, deal, heap, least, meal, neat, seam, ease, bleat

19-3: **e:** he, she, me, be, we

FEATURE 20
Long-I (ī) Words
20-1: **y:** dry, cry, by, shy, sky, my, fly, sly, try, why, sly

20-2: **ye:** bye, dye, rye, eye

20-3: **igh:** bright, fight, sigh, tight, high, light, might, night, right, flight, fright, sight, thigh, slight

20-4: **iCC:** find, kind, bind, blind, climb, mind, wild, grind, hind, sign, wind*

FEATURE 21
Long-O (ō) Words
21-1: **oCC:** cold, hold, old, told, gold, mold, bold, both, fold, roll, scold, bolt, folk, ghost, post, sold, host, stroll, jolt, poll, scroll

21-2: **oa:** boat, coat, float, moat, toast, road, load, toad, coach, croak, coal, groan, foam, oat, roast, throat, soak, goal, boast, loan, oak, coast, soap

21-3: **ow:** grow, show, slow, know, snow, crow, blown, bow*, tow, glow, flown, flow, throw, low, own, grown

FEATURE 22
Long-U (ū) Words
22-1: **ue:** true, hue, due, glue, clue, blue, cue, Tuesday

22-2: **ui:** fruit, suit, bruise, cruise, juice, ruin, suitcase

22-3: **ew:** blew, brew, chew, crew, dew, drew, few, flew, grew, knew, new, pew, screw, stew, threw

22-4: **oo:** too, room, moon, food, mood, proof, scoop, roost, bloom, soon, doom, moo, boo, hoot, droop, coop, shampoo, loop

Use the long vowel word

EXAMPLE EXERCISE FEATURE 18
(child-led)

Step 1: Say, "Can you Stretch & Catch the word **chain**?"

Step 2: Your child will Stretch the word out, putting one finger in the air per sound he/she says: "/**ch**/ [first finger up], /**ā**/ [second finger up], /**n**/ [third finger up]."

Step 3: Next, your child will spell the word by wriggling each finger per letter it represents. Your child will say, "C-H-A-I-N." (When your child spells the word, he/she should wriggle his/her first finger for both the letters **C** and **H** and wriggle the second finger for both letters **A** and **I**.)

Step 4: If your child spelled the word correctly, move to Step 5. If your child was unable to spell the word correctly, move to the bullet point below.

- Say, "What is the long-vowel sound you hear in the word **chain**?" If your child doesn't say it's the /**ā**/, tell him/her: "I hear the /**ā**/ sound in the word **chain**." Move to the next bullet point.
- Say, "What spelling pattern does the word **chain** follow?" You want your child to identify the **ai** spelling pattern. If your child identifies the correct spelling pattern, have him/her Stretch and spell the word again using the spelling pattern and then move to Step 5. If your child is unable to identify the spelling pattern, move to the bullet point below.
- Stretch & Catch the word for him/her. Say, "When I hear the word **chain**, I hear /**ch**/ [first finger up], /**ā**/ [second finger up], /**n**/ [third finger up]. The word **chain** has the **ai** spelling pattern." Then look at your fingers and spell the word correctly for the child: "**Chain** is spelled **C-H** [wriggle/point to first finger], **A-I** [wriggle/point to second finger], **N** [wriggle/point to third finger]." Move to the next bullet point.
- Now have your child Stretch and spell the same word. The child will say, "/**ch**/ [first finger up], /**ā**/ [second finger up], /**n**/ [third finger up]." Next, your child will look at his/her fingers and spell the word: "C-H-A-I-N." (When your child spells the word, he/she should wriggle the first finger for both the letters **C** and **H** and wriggle the second finger for both letters, **A** and **I**.) Move to Step 5.

Step 5: Now have your child Catch the word **chain,** saying it all together quickly and bringing his/her fingers back into a fist.

Optional: Finally, use the note cards to show your child the letters that make up the word, and have him/her manipulate the cards to make the new word. *This is a very helpful activity if your child is having trouble with the spelling pattern.*

Optional: Use word cards to practice the Stretch & Catch Reading Strategy.

EXAMPLE EXERCISE FEATURE 19
(child-led)

Step 1: Say, "Can you Stretch & Catch the word **clean**?"

Step 2: Your child will Stretch the word out, putting one finger in the air per sound he/she says: "/c/ [first finger up], /l/ [second finger up], /ē/ [third finger up], /n/ [fourth finger up]."

Step 3: Next, your child will spell the word by wriggling each finger per letter it represents. Your child will say, "C-L-E-A-N." (In this word, when your child wriggles his/her third finger, he/she will say two letters, **E** and **A**.)

Step 4: If your child spelled the word correctly, move to Step 5. If your child was unable to spell the word correctly, move to the bullet point below.

- Say, "What is the long-vowel sound you hear in the word **clean**?" If your child doesn't say it's the /ē/, tell him/her: "I hear the /ē/ in the word **clean**." Move to the next bullet point.
- Say, "What spelling pattern does the word **clean** follow?" You want your child to identify the **ea** spelling pattern. If your child identifies the correct spelling pattern, have him/her Stretch and spell the word again using the spelling pattern and then move to Step 5. If your child is unable to identify the spelling pattern, move to the bullet point below.
- Stretch & Catch the word for him/her: "When I hear the word **clean**, I hear /c/ [first finger up], /l/ [second finger up], /ē/ [third finger up], /n/ [fourth finger up]. The word **clean** has the **ea** spelling pattern." Now spell the word correctly for your child: "**Clean** is spelled **C** [wriggle/point to first finger], **L** [wriggle/point to second finger], **E-A** [wriggle/point to third finger], **N** [wriggle/point to fourth finger]." Move to the next bullet point.
- Now have your child Stretch and spell the same word. Your child will say, "/c/ [first finger up], /l/ [second finger up], /ē/ [third finger up], /n/ [fourth finger up]." Next, your child will look at his/her fingers and spell the word: "C-L-E-A-N." (When your child spells the word, he/she should wriggle the third finger for both letters, **E** and **A**.) Move to Step 5.

Step 5: Now have your child Catch the word, saying it all together quickly and bringing his/her fingers back into a fist.

Optional: Finally, use the note cards to show your child the letters that make up the word, and have him/her manipulate the cards to make the new word. *This is a very helpful activity if your child is having trouble with the spelling pattern.*

Optional: Use word cards to practice the Stretch & Catch Reading Strategy.

EXAMPLE EXERCISE FEATURE 20
(child-led)

Step 1: Say, "Can you Stretch & Catch the word **blind**?"

Step 2: Your child will Stretch the word out, putting one finger in the air per sound he/she says: "/**b**/ [first finger up], /**l**/ [second finger up], /ī/ [third finger up], /**n**/ [fourth finger up], /**d**/ [fifth finger up]."

Step 3: Next, your child will spell the word. Your child will say, "**B-L-I-N-D**." (When your child spells the word, he/she should wriggle a finger per letter for this word.)

Step 4: If your child spelled the word correctly, move to Step 5. If your child was unable to spell the word correctly, move to the bullet point below.

- Say, "What is the long-vowel sound you hear in the word **blind**?" If your child doesn't say it's the /ī/, tell him/her: "I hear the /ī/ in the word **blind**." Move to the next bullet point.
- Say, "What spelling pattern does the word **blind** follow?" You want your child to identify the **iCC (i/consonant/consonant)** spelling pattern. If your child identifies the correct spelling pattern, have him/her Stretch and spell the word again using the spelling pattern and then move to Step 5. If your child is unable to identify the spelling pattern move to the bullet point below.
- Stretch & Catch the word for him/her. Say, "When I hear the word **blind**, I hear /**b**/ [first finger up], /**l**/ [second finger up], /ī/ [third finger up], /**n**/ [fourth finger up], /**d**/ [fifth finger up]. The word **blind** has the **iCC** spelling pattern." Then look at your fingers and spell the word correctly for your child: "**Blind** is spelled **B** [wriggle/point to first finger], **L** [wriggle/point to second finger], **I** [wriggle/point to third finger], **N** [wriggle/point to fourth finger], **D** [wriggle/point to fifth finger]." Move to the next bullet point.
- Now have your child Stretch and spell the same word. The child will say, "/**b**/ [first finger up], /**l**/ [second finger up], /ī/ [third finger up], /**n**/ [fourth finger up], /**d**/ [fifth finger up]." Next your child will look at his/her fingers and spell the word: "**B-L-I-N-D**." (When your child spells the word, he/she should wriggle each finger that represents each letter.) Move to Step 5.

Step 5: Now have your child Catch the word **blind**, by saying it all together quickly and bringing his/her fingers back into a fist.

Optional: Finally, use the note cards to show your child the letters that make up the word, and have him/her manipulate the cards to make the new word. *This is a very helpful activity if your child is having trouble with the spelling pattern.*

Optional: Use word cards to practice the Stretch & Catch Reading Strategy.

EXAMPLE EXERCISE FEATURE 21
(child-led)

Step 1: Say, "Can you Stretch & Catch the word **grow**?"

Step 2: Your child will Stretch the word out, putting one finger in the air per sound he/she says: "/**g**/ [first finger up], /**r**/ [second finger up], /**ō**/ [third finger up]."

Step 3: Next your child will spell the word. Your child will say, "**G-R-O-W**." (When your child spells the word, he/she should wriggle his/her third finger for both letters, **O** and **W**.)

Step 4: If your child spells the word correctly, move to Step 5. If your child is unable to spell the word correctly, move to the bullet point below.

- Say, "What is the long-vowel sound you hear in the word **grow**?" If your child doesn't say it's the /**ō**/, tell him/her: "I hear the /**ō**/ in the word **grow**." Move to the next bullet point.
- Say, "What spelling pattern does the word **grow** follow?" You want your child to identify the **ow** spelling pattern. If your child identifies the correct spelling pattern have him/her Stretch and spell the word again using the spelling pattern and then move to Step 5. If your child is unable to identify the spelling pattern move to the bullet point below.
- Stretch & Catch the word for him/her, "When I hear the word **grow**, I hear /**g**/ [first finger up], /**r**/ [second finger up], /**ō**/ [third finger up]. The word **grow** has the **ow** spelling pattern." Then look at your fingers and spell the word correctly for your child, "**Grow** is spelled **G** [wriggle/point to first finger], **R** [wriggle/point to second finger], **O-W** [wriggle/point to third finger.]" Move to the next bullet point.
- Now have your child Stretch and spell the same word. The child will say, "/**g**/ [first finger up], /**r**/ [second finger up], /**ō**/ [third finger up]." Next your child will look at his/her fingers and spell the word: "**G-R-O-W**." (When your child spells the word, he/she should wriggle the third finger for both the letters **O** and **W**.) Move to Step 5.

Step 5: Now have your child Catch the word **grow**, saying it all together quickly and bringing his/her fingers back into a fist.

Optional: Finally, use the note cards to show your child the letters that make up the word, and have him/her manipulate the cards to make the new word. *This is a very helpful activity if your child is having trouble with the spelling pattern.*

Optional: Use word cards to practice the Stretch & Catch Reading Strategy.

EXAMPLE EXERCISE FEATURE 22
(child-led)

Step 1: Say, "Can you Stretch & Catch the word **new**?"

Step 2: Have your child Stretch the word out, putting one finger in the air per sound he/she says: "/**n**/ [first finger up], /**ū**/ [second finger up]."

Step 3: Next, your child will spell the word. Your child will say, "**N-E-W**." (When your child spells the word, he/she should wriggle the second finger, for both letters **E** and **W**.)

Step 4: If your child spells the word correctly, move to Step 5. If your child was unable to spell the word correctly, move to the bullet point below.

- Say, "What is the long-vowel sound you hear in the word **new**?" If your child doesn't say it's /**ū**/, tell him/her: "I hear the /**ū**/ in the word **new**."
- Ask, "What spelling pattern does the word **new** follow?" You want your child to identify the **ew** spelling pattern. If your child identifies the correct spelling pattern, have him/her Stretch and spell the word again using the spelling pattern and then move to Step 5. If your child is unable to identify the spelling pattern move to the bullet point below.
- Stretch & Catch the word for him/her: "When I hear the word **new**, I hear /**n**/ [first finger up], /**ū**/ [second finger up]. The word **new** has the **ew** spelling pattern." Then look at your fingers and spell the word correctly for your child: "**New** is spelled **N** [wriggle/point to first finger], **E-W** [wriggle/point to second finger]." Move to the next bullet point.
- Now have your child Stretch and spell the same word. The child will say, "/**n**/ [first finger up], /**ū**/ [second finger up]." Next, your child will look at his/her fingers and spell the word: "**N-E-W**." (When your child spells the word, he/she should wriggle the second finger for both the letters **E** and **W**.) Move to Step 5.

Step 5: Now have your child Catch the word **new**, by saying it all together quickly and bringing his/her fingers back into a fist.

Optional: Finally, use the note cards to show your child the letters that make up the word, and have him/her manipulate the cards to make the new word. *This is a very helpful activity if your child is having trouble with the spelling pattern.*

Optional: Use word cards to practice the Stretch & Catch Reading Strategy.

CHAPTER EIGHT

DIPHTHONGS

DAILY READING

Continue to encourage your child to read daily. Make sure your child is choosing books with topics that interest him/her. If your child is struggling with fluency, have him/her read books that are at an easier level. This will help your child read more fluently because he/she will be able to read all of the words within the text without struggling. At this point, the TWL words should be automatic for your child, but if they are not, continue working on them so they do become automatic; this will also help with your child's fluency because when a child automatically recognizes and reads TWL words, he/she doesn't have to stop (to sound out words) so often. The more words and spelling patterns your child knows automatically, the more likely he/she will read fluently and read higher-level books.

STRETCH & CATCH DIPHTHONGS

Now that your child has mastered long vowels, you will introduce four diphthong spelling patterns. A diphthong is formed when two vowels glide together to make a new and distinct sound. (The di- in the word *diphthong* means two.) For example, when you say the words *toy* and *coin,* notice that the **oy** and **oi** spelling patterns make the same diphthong sound. Similarly, the **ow** and **ou** spelling patterns both make the same sound, as in *cow* and *house.* Notice that your mouth moved in two places when you said the diphthong sounds /**oy**/, /**oi**/, /**ow**/, /**ou**/. I suggest teaching the **oy** and **oi** spelling patterns together and then the **ow** and **ou** spelling patterns together. When you discuss the /**oy**/ sound, you can explain that he/she should use the **oi** spelling pattern if the sound is in the middle of the word and use the **oy** spelling pattern if the sound is at the end of the word. The **ow** and **ou** spelling patterns are similar: The /**ow**/ sound in the middle of a word is typically spelled with the **ou** spelling pattern, and at the end of a word, it is spelled with the **ow** spelling pattern.

Although there are many theories about how many sounds are in a diphthong, in this book, we look at diphthongs as two letters that glide together to make one sound. Diphthongs are therefore like digraphs in that they contain two letters and one new sound. The difference between the digraph and the diphthong is that when a person says a diphthong, the mouth makes two movements, whereas saying a digraph makes only one movement in the mouth.

This is the first chapter with no TWL words for your child to master. Continue working on any TWL words that your child does not know automatically or any TWL words you think your child should review.

Remember, after your child has completed the words within this feature, you can use the assessment tool in Chapter One to determine if he/she can move on to the next feature. Remember also that 80% is mastery within each feature, but you may choose to stay in a feature for as long as your child needs. At any time, you can move on to the next feature if your child scored lower than 80% if you feel he/she does well during your lessons. You can decide when your child is ready to move to the next feature.

This chapter uses only child-led Stretch & Catch templates.

OPTIONAL TEMPLATE FOR INTRODUCING FEATURE 23

*I recommend using note cards to introduce the diphthong before each lesson. If you do not have time to do this step, it is okay; you will just explain it during your Stretch & Catch lesson. If you do have time for the introductory note cards, simply create a note card with a word from the feature your child is being introduced to. For example, if you are introducing Feature 23, lesson 1 (23-1), you can use the word **toy**.*

Step 1: Place the diphthong word on the table.

Step 2: Say, "Do you notice anything about this word?" Encourage your child to notice the **diphthong** in the word.

Step 3: Say, "I'm going to Stretch & Catch this word for you."

Step 4: Stretch & Catch the word: "(**First sound**) [first finger up], (**diphthong sound**) [second finger up]."

Step 5: Now Catch the word.

Step 6: Say, "Did you notice that the (**diphthong sound**) only made one sound but your mouth moved two places?" Have your child say the diphthong sound. Then tell him/her the spelling pattern and the spelling rule for that spelling pattern.

Step 7: Now have your child Stretch & Catch the same word.

Step 8: Next, tell the child that he/she will be Stretching & Catching more words with this diphthong.

TEMPLATE FEATURE 23
(child-led Stretch & Catch)

(DIPHTHONG IN THE MIDDLE OF THE WORD)

Step 1: Say, "Can you Stretch & Catch the word (**word**)?"

Step 2: Have your child Stretch the word out, putting one finger in the air per sound he/she says. (Remember, your child will lift only one finger per diphthong sound even though there are two letters per sound.)

Step 3: Now have your child look at his/her fingers and spell the word.

Step 4: If your child spells the diphthong word correctly, move to Step 5. If your child is unable to spell the word correctly, move to the bullet point below.

- Say, "What is the diphthong sound you hear in the word (**word**)?" If your child doesn't say the correct diphthong sound, say, "I hear the diphthong (**diphthong sound**) sound in the word (**word**)." Move to the next bullet point.
- Say, "Is this (**diphthong sound**) sound in the middle or at the end of the word (**word**)?" You want your child to recognize where the diphthong sound is within the word so he/she will identify the correct spelling pattern to use for the word. If your child gets this correct, great; move to the bullet point below. If not, say, "When I say the word (**word**), I hear the diphthong in the **middle** of the word." Move to the next bullet point.
- Now say, "If this diphthong sound is in the **middle** of the word (**word**), which spelling pattern does the word (**word**) follow?" You want your child to identify the (**diphthong spelling pattern**) spelling pattern because it's at the **middle** of the word. If your child identifies the correct spelling pattern, have him/her Stretch and spell the word again using the spelling pattern and then move to Step 5. If your child is unable to identify the spelling pattern move to the bullet point below.
- Identify the spelling pattern for him/her: "The diphthong is in the **middle** of this word, so I know to use the (**spelling pattern**) spelling pattern." Next, Stretch the word, lifting one finger per sound in the word. Finally, spell the word for your child: "(**Word**) is spelled (**spelling of word**)." (Wriggle/point to a finger for each sound as you spell the word correctly for your child, keeping in mind that some fingers will represent two letters, and emphasize the diphthong with the appropriate finger.) Move to the next bullet point.
- Now have your child Stretch and spell the same word, putting one finger up with each sound. Then have him/her look at his/her fingers and spell the word. Move to Step 5.

Step 5: Now have your child Catch the word by saying it all together quickly and bringing his/her fingers back into a fist.

Optional: Finally, use the note cards to show your child the letters that make up the word, and have him/her manipulate the cards to make the new word. *This is a very helpful activity if your child is having trouble with the spelling pattern.*

Optional: Use word cards to practice the Stretch & Catch Reading Strategy.

TEMPLATE FEATURE 23
(child-led Stretch & Catch)

(DIPHTHONG AT THE END OF THE WORD)

Step 1: Say, "Can you Stretch & Catch the word (**word**)?"

Step 2: Have your child Stretch the word out, putting one finger in the air per sound he/she says. (Remember, he/she will lift only one finger per diphthong sound even though there are two letters per sound.)

Step 3: Now have your child look at his/her fingers and spell the word.

Step 4: If your child spells the diphthong word correctly, move to Step 5. If your child is unable to spell the word correctly, move to the bullet point below.

- Say, "What is the diphthong sound you hear in the word (**word**)?" If your child doesn't say the correct diphthong sound, say, "I hear the diphthong (**diphthong sound**) sound in the word (**word**)." Move to the next bullet point.
- Say, "Is this (**diphthong sound**) sound in the middle or at the end of the word (**word**)?" You want your child to recognize where the diphthong sound is within the word so he/she will identify the correct spelling pattern to use for the word. If your child gets it correct, great; move to the bullet point below. If not, say, "When I say the word (**word**), I hear the diphthong at the **end** of the word." Move to the next bullet point.
- Now say, "If this diphthong sound is at the **end** of the word (**word**), which spelling pattern does the word (**word**) follow?" You want your child to identify the (**diphthong spelling pattern**) spelling pattern because it's at the **end** of the word. If your child identifies the correct spelling pattern, have him/her Stretch and spell the word again using the spelling pattern and then move to Step 5. If your child is unable to identify the spelling pattern move to the bullet point below.
- Say, "The diphthong is at the **end** of this word, so I know to use the (**spelling pattern**) spelling pattern." Next, Stretch the word, lifting one finger per sound in the word. Finally, spell the word for your child: "(**Word**) is spelled (**spelling of word**)." (Wriggle/point to a finger for each sound as you spell the word correctly for your child, keeping in mind that some fingers will represent two letters, and emphasize the diphthong with the appropriate finger.) Move to the next bullet point.
- Now have your child Stretch and spell the same word, putting one finger up with each sound. Then have him/her look at his/her fingers and spell the word. Move to Step 5.

Step 5: Now have your child Catch the word by saying it all together quickly and bringing his/her fingers back into a fist.

Optional: Finally, use the note cards to show your child the letters that make up the word, and have him/her manipulate the cards to make the new word. *This is a very helpful activity if your child is having trouble with the spelling pattern.*

Optional: Use word cards to practice the Stretch & Catch Reading Strategy.

LESSONS FOR FEATURE 23

FEATURE 23

23-1: **oy**: toy, boy, joy, soy, enjoy, ploy, coy, troy, ahoy

23-2: **oi**: oil, coin, join, oink, noise, soil, moist, voice, avoid

23-3: **ow**: cow, bow, now, plow, how, down, owl, frown, clown, brown, drown, chow

23-4: **ou**: shout, count, mound, round, sound, our, ouch, couch, house, pound, ground, about, mouth

EXAMPLE EXERCISE FEATURE 23
(child-led)

(DIPHTHONG IN THE MIDDLE OF THE WORD)

Step 1: Says, "Can you Stretch & Catch the word **coin**?"

Step 2: Have your child Stretch the word out, putting one finger in the air per sound he/she says: "/c/ [first finger up], /oi/ [second finger up], /n/ [third finger up]." (Remember, he/she will lift only one finger per diphthong sound, even though there are two letters per sound.)

Step 3: Now have your child look at his/her fingers and spell the word.

Step 4: If your child spells the diphthong word correctly, move to Step 5. If your child is unable to spell the word correctly, move to the bullet point below.

- Say, "What is the diphthong sound you hear in the word **coin**?" If your child doesn't say it's /oi/, tell him/her: "I hear the diphthong /oi/ sound in the word **coin**."
- Say, "Is this /oi/ sound in the middle or at the end of the word **coin**?" You want your child to recognize where the diphthong sound is within the word so he/she will identify the correct spelling pattern to use for this word. If your child gets it correct, great; move to the bullet point below. If not, say, "When I say the word **coin**, I hear the diphthong in the **middle** of the word." Move to the next bullet point.
- Now say, "If this diphthong sound is in the **middle** of the word **coin,** which spelling pattern does the word **coin** follow?" You want your child to identify that it's the **oi** spelling pattern because it's in the middle of the word. If your child identifies the correct spelling pattern, have him/her Stretch and spell the word again using the spelling pattern and then move to Step 5. If your child is unable to identify the spelling pattern move to the next bullet point.
- Identify the spelling pattern for him/her: "The diphthong is in the **middle** of this word, so I know to use the **oi** spelling pattern." Next, Stretch the word for your child: "When I hear the word **coin**, I hear /c/ [first finger up], /oi/ [second finger up], /n/ [third finger up]." Now look at your fingers and wriggle/point to each finger as you spell the word, keeping in mind that some fingers will represent two letters, and emphasizing the diphthong with the second finger: "**Coin** is spelled **C-O-I-N**." Finally, Catch the word for your child by saying the word quickly and bringing all your fingers into a fist.
- Now have your child Stretch and spell the same word, putting one finger up with each sound. Then have him/her look at his/her fingers and spell the word. Move to Step 5.

Step 5: Now have your child Catch the word by saying it all together quickly and bringing his/her fingers back into a fist.

Optional: Finally, use the note cards to show your child the letters that make up the word, and have him/her manipulate the cards to make the new word. *This is a very helpful activity if your child is having trouble with the spelling pattern.*

Optional: Use word cards to practice the Stretch & Catch Reading Strategy.

EXAMPLE EXERCISE FEATURE 23
(child-led)

(DIPHTHONG AT THE END OF THE WORD)

Step 1: Say, "Can you Stretch & Catch the word **cow**?"

Step 2: Have your child Stretch the word out, putting one finger in the air per sound he/she says: "/c/ [first finger up], /ow/ [second finger up]." (Remember, he/she will lift only one finger per diphthong sound, even though there are two letters per sound.)

Step 3: Now have your child look at his/her fingers and spell the word.

Step 4: If your child spells the diphthong word correctly, move to Step 5. If your child is unable to spell the word correctly, move to the bullet point below.

- Say, "What is the diphthong sound you hear in the word **cow**?" If your child doesn't say it's the diphthong /**ow**/, tell him/her: "I hear the diphthong /**ow**/ sound in the word **cow**."
- Say, "Is this /**ow**/ sound in the middle or at the end of the word **cow**?" [You want your child to recognize where the diphthong sound is within the word so he/she will identify the correct spelling pattern to use for this word. If your child gets it correct, great; move to the bullet point below. If not, say, "When I say the word **cow**, I hear the diphthong at the **end** of the word." Move to the next bullet point.
- Now say, "If this diphthong sound is at the **end** of the word **cow**, which spelling pattern does the word **cow** follow?" You want your child to identify that it's the **ow** spelling pattern because it's at the **end** of the word. If your child identifies the correct spelling pattern, have him/her Stretch and spell the word again using the spelling pattern and then move to Step 5. If your child is unable to identify the spelling pattern, move to the bullet point below.
- Identify the spelling pattern for him/her: "The diphthong is at the **end** of this word, so I know to use the **ow** spelling pattern." Next, Stretch the word for your child: "When I hear the word **cow**, I hear /c/ [first finger up], /ow/ [second finger up]." Now look at your fingers and wriggle/point to each finger, keeping in mind that the second finger will represent two letters, and emphasizing the diphthong with the second finger: "**Cow** is spelled **C-O-W**." Finally, Catch the word for your child by saying the word quickly and bringing all your fingers into a fist.
- Now have your child Stretch and spell the same word, putting one finger up with each sound. Then have him/her look at his/her fingers and spell the word. Move to Step 5.

Step 5: Now have your child Catch the word **cow** by saying it all together quickly and bringing his/her fingers back into a fist.

Optional: Finally, use the note cards to show your child the letters that make up the word, and have him/her manipulate the cards to make the new word. *This is a very helpful activity if your child is having trouble with the spelling pattern.*

Optional: Use word cards to practice the Stretch & Catch Reading Strategy.

CHAPTER NINE

R-CONTROLLED VOWEL PATTERNS

DAILY READING

A great reader is one who reads often. The more a child reads, the better reader the child will become. Continue encouraging your child to read silently. Now that your child is reading silently to himself/herself, make sure to occasionally ask him/her to read a chapter aloud to you so you can be sure your child is using the Stretch & Catch Reading Strategy. It is also important that your child continue to use the five-finger test from Chapter One to see if the book he/she is reading is at the appropriate level. Occasionally listening to your child read and watching him/her use the five-finger test will help you know if your child is picking "just right" books.

STRETCH & CATCH R-CONTROLLED VOWEL PATTERNS

In this final chapter, we dive deep into **R**-controlled word patterns. When a vowel is followed by the letter **R**, the letter **R** takes over the vowel sound by "controlling" it and making a new sound; thus, **R**-controlled vowel patterns.

At this point, your child has mastered many different spelling patterns and TWL words. You will continue to use child-led Stretch & Catch templates. When introducing **R**-controlled vowel patterns, I make suggestions on whether to introduce the **R**-controlled vowel pattern by itself or with another **R**-controlled vowel pattern. The ultimate decision whether you introduce spelling patterns by themselves or with multiple spelling patterns, however, is strictly dependent on your child's instructional level. You do not want to overwhelm your child by introducing many spelling patterns at one time, but you also want your child to work at his/her instructional level.

I sometimes suggest introducing more than one spelling pattern at a time because two or more of the patterns make the same sound or follow the same guidelines; this ultimately can help your child know when to use each spelling pattern. **R**-controlled vowel patterns are difficult because there are not many helpful guidelines to help a child figure out which vowel pattern belongs in which word. For most of the **R**-controlled vowel patterns, the child must memorize which **R**-controlled vowel pattern fits within each word. Your child will be able to memorize these patterns within each word by using the introductory note cards for each feature, Stretching & Catching **R**-controlled words daily, using the Stretch & Catch Reading Strategy, and by using the letter note cards to make his/her new **R**-controlled words.

FEATURE GUIDELINES FOR EACH SPELLING PATTERN

You will want to teach your child the following rule: "When we see the pattern of a vowel or vowels, followed by the letter **R**, the letter **R** takes over the vowel sound by controlling it and making a new sound." We will discuss the following spelling patterns for **R**-controlled vowels: **-ar, -are, -air, -ear, -eer, -er, -ur, -ir, -or**.

The guidelines for spelling **R**-controlled vowel words do not always help a child know which **R**-controlled vowel pattern to use in each word; therefore, the more you immerse your child in many **R**-controlled vowel-patterned words, the more chances he/she has to memorize which spelling pattern fits within each word. The following guidelines will help you teach **R**-controlled vowel patterns to your child.

Please keep in mind that these guidelines are to be helpful hints for spelling **R**-controlled words but that there are always exceptions in words within the English language.

FEATURE 24

R-Controlled Vowel Patterns -ar, -are, -air (/**ar**/ versus /**air**/) (Teach the **-ar** pattern by itself. Teach **-are** and **-air** together.)

- *-ar:* When we see the pattern of a vowel **A** followed by the letter **R**, the letter **R** takes over the vowel sound by controlling it and making a new sound. For example, *car.*
- *-are:* When we see the pattern of a vowel **A** followed by the letter **R**, the letter **R** takes over the vowel sound by controlling it and making a new sound. In this case, the letter **R** is also followed by the vowel **E**. For example, *care.*
- *-air:* When we see the pattern of two vowels **A** and **I** followed by the letter **R**, the letter **R** takes over the vowel sounds by controlling it and making a new sound. For example, *stair.*

  *The guideline for the **-are** and **-air** patterns are taught together so the child can see that although they make the same sound, they are spelled differently.*

FEATURE 25
R-Controlled Vowel Patterns -ear, -eer (/**ear**/) (Teach **-ear** and **-eer** together.)

- When we see the pattern of two vowels followed by the letter **R**, the letter **R** takes over the vowel sound by controlling it and making a new sound. For example, *near, deer.*

  *The **-ear** and **-eer** patterns are taught together so the child can see that although they make the same sound, they are spelled differently.*

FEATURE 26
R-Controlled Vowel Patterns –or, -er, -ur, -ir, (/**or**/ versus /**er**/) (Teach **-or** by itself. Teach **-er**, **-ur**, and **-ir** together.)

- When we see a vowel **O** followed by the letter **R**, the letter **R** takes over the vowel sound by controlling it and making a new sound. For example, *corn.*
- When we see a vowel **E**, **U**, or **I** followed by the letter **R**, the letter **R** takes over the vowel sound by controlling it and making a new sound. For example, *her, surf, bird.*

  *The **-er**, **-ur**, and **-ir** spelling patterns are taught together so the child can see that although they make the same sound, they are spelled differently.*

Remember that after your child has completed the words within each feature, you can use the assessment tool in Chapter One to decide if he/she can move on to the next feature. Remember also that 80% is mastery within each feature, but you may choose to stay in a feature for as long as your child needs. You can move on to the next feature if your child scored lower than 80% on the assessment if you feel he/she does well during your lessons. You choose when your child is ready to move to the next feature.

OPTIONAL TEMPLATE FOR INTRODUCING FEATURES 24–26

*I recommend using note cards to introduce the **R**-controlled vowels before each lesson. If you do not have time to do this step, it is okay; you will just explain it during your Stretch & Catch lesson. If you do have time for the introductory note cards, simply write an **R**-controlled word from the feature your child is being introduced to on a note card. For example, if you are introducing Feature 24, Lesson 1 (24-1): **-ar** words, you can use the word **barn**.*

Step 1: Place the **R**-controlled vowel word on the table.

Step 2: Say, "Do you notice anything about this word?" Encourage your child to notice that there is an **R**-controlled spelling pattern in the word.

Step 3: Say, "I'm going to Stretch & Catch this word for you."

Step 4: Say, "(**First sound**) [first finger up], (**R-controlled vowel sound**) [second finger up], (**ending sound**) [third finger up]."

Step 5: Now Catch the word, saying it quickly while you bring your fingers into a fist.

Step 6: Say, "Did you notice that the (**spelling pattern**) only made one sound?"

Step 7: Now have your child Stretch & Catch the same word.

Step 8: Finally, tell your child that he/she will be Stretching & Catching more words with this spelling pattern.

TEMPLATE FEATURES 24–26
(child-led Stretch & Catch)

Step 1: Say, "Can you Stretch & Catch the word (**word**)?"

Step 2: Have your child Stretch the word out, putting one finger in the air per sound he/she says. (Remember, he/she will lift only one finger per **R**-controlled vowel sound even though there are more letters per sound.)

Step 3: Next, have your child look at his/her fingers and spell the word.

Step 4: If your child spells the **R**-controlled word correctly, move to Step 5. If your child is unable to spell the word correctly, move to the bullet point below.

- Say, "What is the **R**-controlled vowel sound you hear in the word (**word**)?" If your child doesn't say the **R**-controlled sound, tell him/her: "I hear the (**R-controlled sound**) sound in the word (**word**)." Move to next bullet point.
- Say, "What spelling pattern does the word (**word**) follow?" If your child identifies the correct spelling pattern, have him/her Stretch and spell the word again using the spelling pattern and then move to Step 5. If your child is unable to identify the spelling pattern move to the bullet point below.
- Stretch the word for him/her, lifting one finger per sound in the word. Then remind your child of the spelling pattern for the word by wriggling/pointing to the correct finger to emphasize the **R**-controlled sound, saying, "The word (**word**) has the (**spelling pattern**) spelling pattern." Next, spell the word correctly for your child, wriggling/pointing to one finger for each sound: "(**Word**) is spelled (**spelling of word**)." Finally, Catch the word, saying it quickly as you pull your fingers into a fist. Move to the next bullet point.
- Now have your child Stretch and spell the same word, putting one finger up with each sound. Then have your child look at his/her fingers and spell the word. Move to Step 5.

Step 5: Now have your child Catch the word, saying it all together quickly and bringing his/her fingers back into a fist.

Optional: Finally, use the note cards to show your child the letters that make up the word, and have him/her manipulate the cards to make the new word. *This is a very helpful activity if your child is having trouble with the spelling pattern.*

Optional: Use word cards to practice the Stretch & Catch Reading Strategy.

LESSONS FOR FEATURES 24–26

FEATURE 24: R-CONTROLLED PATTERNS

24:1: **-ar**: carp, bar, star, car, dark, far, part, start, arm, card, art, cart, par, tar, scar, ajar, charm, harm, yard, hard, dart, scarf

24:2: **-air**: chair, hair, pair, stair, flair, repair, staircase, dairy, fairy, airport

24:3: **-are**: care, scare, share, stare, dare, flare, glare, rare, square, fare, hare

FEATURE 25: R-CONTROLLED PATTERNS

25:1: **-ear**: near, clear, dear, fear, year, gear, rear, ear, pear

25:2: **-eer**: beer, deer, peer, sheer, seer, cheer, steer, sneer, career, volunteer

FEATURE 26: R-CONTROLLED PATTERNS

26:1: **-er**: her, herd, jerk, perch, germ, perk, stern, term, nerd, after, taller, louder, faster

26:2: **-ur**: surf, hurt, burn, curl, fur, turn, church, churn, curb, return, spur, blur

26:3: **-ir**: bird, first, girl, dirt, chirp, third, birth, shirt, firm, stir, thirsty, skirt, thirty

26: 4: **-or**: for, corn, born, north, short, cord, worn, storm, torch, pork, lord, fort, horse, absorb, acorn, thorn, sport, hornet, form, stork

EXAMPLE EXERCISE FEATURE 24
(child-led)

Step 1: Say, "Can you Stretch & Catch the word **far**?"

Step 2: Have your child Stretch the word out, putting one finger in the air per sound he/she says: "/**f**/ [first finger up], /**ar**/ [second finger up]." (Remember, he/she will lift only one finger per **R**-controlled vowel sound even though there are more letters per sound.)

Step 3: Now have your child look at his/her fingers and spell the word: "**F-A-R.**"

Step 4: If your child spells the **R**-controlled word correctly, move to Step 5. If your child is unable to spell the word correctly, move to the bullet point below.

- Say, "What is the **R**-controlled vowel sound you hear in the word **far**?" If your child doesn't say that it's the **R**-controlled /**ar**/ sound, tell him/her: "I hear the **R**-controlled /**ar**/ sound in the word **far**." Move to the next bullet point.
- Say, "What spelling pattern does the word **far** follow?" You want your child to identify the -**ar** spelling pattern. If your child identifies the correct spelling pattern, have him/her Stretch and spell the word again using the spelling pattern and then move to Step 5. If your child is unable to identify the spelling pattern move to the bullet point below.
- Stretch the word for him/her: "When I hear the word **far**, I hear /**f**/ [first finger up], /**ar**/ [second finger up]." Then remind your child of the spelling pattern for the word by wriggling/pointing to the second finger to emphasize the **R**-controlled sound, saying, "The word **far** has the -**ar** spelling pattern." Now spell the word correctly for your child: "**Far** is spelled **F** [wriggle/point to first finger], **A-R** [wriggle/point to second finger]." Finally, Catch the word by saying it quickly and bringing your fingers into a fist. Move to the next bullet point.
- Now have your child Stretch and spell the same word: "/**f**/ [first finger up], /**ar**/ [second finger up]." Next, have your child look at his/her fingers and spell the word. Move to Step 5.

Step 5: Now have your child Catch the word **far** by saying it all together quickly and bringing his/her fingers back into a fist.

Optional: Finally, use the note cards to show your child the letters that make up the word, and have him/her manipulate the cards to make the new word. *This is a very helpful activity if your child is having trouble with the spelling pattern.*

Optional: Use word cards to practice the Stretch & Catch Reading Strategy.

EXAMPLE EXERCISE FEATURE 25
(child-led)

Step 1: Say, "Can you Stretch & Catch the word **dear**?"

Step 2: Have your child Stretch the word out, putting one finger in the air per sound he/she says: "/**d**/ [first finger up], /**ear**/ [second finger up]." (Remember, your child will lift only one finger per **R**-controlled vowel sound even though there are more letters per sound.)

Step 3: Now have your child look at his/her fingers and spell the word, "D-E-A-R."

Step 4: If your child spells the word correctly, move to Step 5. If your child is unable to spell the word correctly, move to the bullet point below.

- Say, "What is the **R**-controlled vowel sound you hear in the word **dear**?" If your child doesn't say that it's the **R**-controlled /**ear**/ sound, tell him/her: "I hear the **R**-controlled /**ear**/ sound in the word **dear**."
- Say, "What spelling pattern does the word **dear** follow?" You want your child to identify the -**ear** spelling pattern. If your child identifies the correct spelling pattern, have him/her Stretch and spell the word again using the spelling pattern and move to Step 5. If your child is unable to identify the spelling pattern move to the bullet point below.
- Stretch the word for him/her: "When I hear the word **dear**, I hear /**d**/ [first finger up], /**ear**/ [second finger up]." Then remind your child of the spelling pattern for the word by wriggling/pointing to the second finger to emphasize the **R**-controlled sound, saying, "The word **dear** has the -**ear** spelling pattern." Now spell the word correctly for your child: "**Dear** is spelled **D** [wriggle/point to first finger], **E-A-R** [wriggle/point to second finger]. Finally, Catch the word by saying it quickly and bringing your fingers into a fist. Move to the next bullet point.
- Now have your child Stretch and spell the same word: "/**d**/ [first finger up], /**ear**/ [second finger up]." Next, have your child look at his/her fingers and spell the word. Move to Step 5.

Step 5: Now have your child Catch the word **dear** by saying it all together quickly and bringing his/her fingers back into a fist.

Optional: Finally, use the note cards to show your child the letters that make up the word, and have him/her manipulate the cards to make the new word. *This is a very helpful activity if your child is having trouble with the spelling pattern.*

Optional: Use word cards to practice the Stretch & Catch Reading Strategy.

EXAMPLE EXERCISE FEATURE 26
(child-led)

Step 1: Says, "Can you Stretch & Catch the word **corn**?"

Step 2: Have your child Stretch the word out, putting one finger in the air per sound he/she says: "/c/ [first finger up], /or/ [second finger up], /n/ [third finger up]." (Remember, your child will lift only one finger per **R**-controlled vowel sound even though there are more letters per sound.)

Step 3: Now have your child look at his/her fingers and spell the word.

Step 4: If your child spells the word correctly, move to Step 5. If your child is unable to spell the word correctly, move to the bullet point below.

- Say, "What is the **R**-controlled vowel sound you hear in the word **corn**?" If your child doesn't say that it's the **R**-controlled /or/ sound, tell him her: "I hear the **R**-controlled /or/ sound in the word **corn**." Move to the next bullet point.
- Say, "What spelling pattern does the word **corn** follow?" You want your child to identify the **-or** spelling pattern. If your child identifies the correct spelling pattern, have him/her Stretch and spell the word again using the spelling pattern and then move to Step 5. If your child is unable to identify the spelling pattern move to the bullet point below.
- Stretch the word for him/her: "When I hear the word **corn**, I hear /c/ [first finger up], /or/ [second finger up], /n/ [third finger up]." Then remind your child of the spelling pattern for the word by wriggling/pointing to the second finger to emphasize the **R**-controlled sound, saying, "The word **corn** has the **-or** spelling pattern." Now spell the word correctly for your child: "**Corn** is spelled **C** [wriggle/point to first finger], **O-R** [wriggle/point to second finger], **N** [wriggle/point to third finger]." Move to the next bullet point.
- Now have your child Stretch and spell the same word: "/c/ [first finger up], /or/ [second finger up], /n/ [third finger up]." Next, have your child look at his/her fingers and spell the word. Move to Step 5.

Step 5: Now have your child Catch the word **corn** by saying it all together quickly and bringing his/her fingers back into a fist.

Optional: Finally, use the note cards to show your child the letters that make up the word, and have him/her manipulate the cards to make the new word. *This is a very helpful activity if your child is having trouble with the spelling pattern.*

Optional: Use word cards to practice the Stretch & Catch Reading Strategy.

APPENDIX

MATERIALS FOR INTRODUCING FEATURES 14–17

ă/ā	ĭ/ī	ŏ/ō	ŭ/ū
cat/Cate	kit/kite	hop/hope	cut/cute
bat/bate	bit/bite	cop/cope	cub/cube
mat/mate	grip/gripe	slop/slope	tub/tube
tap/tape	rip/ripe	pop/pope	hug/huge
cap/cape	hid/hide	rob/robe	dud/dude
plan/plane	Tim/time	not/note	us/use
fat/fate	fin/fine	mop/mope	plum/plume
stat/state	rid/ride	dot/dote	
rat/rate	bin/bine	rod/rode	
pan/pane	lit/lite	con/cone	
van/vane	sit/site	cod/code	
man/mane	slid/slide	tot/tote	
Jan/Jane	spit/spite	lob/lobe	
gap/gape	hid/hide		
nap/nape	shin/shine		

FURTHER RESOURCES: LEVELED BOOKS

Many companies sell leveled books. The following are just a few of the places where I found leveled books for my own students and children. You can also search the Internet or go to your local library to find more leveled books.

www.scholastic.com
www.amazon.com
www.pbs.org
http://www.seussville.com/#/books
www.arbookfind.com

ABOUT THE AUTHOR

AMANDA MCNAMARA LOWE has always loved the challenge of teaching children to read. As she became a parent, she realized that other parents were overwhelmed when they attempted to teach their own children to read. The culmination of teaching regular education, special education, college, and her own children for 14 years led her to develop a multi-sensory and developmentally appropriate method called Stretch & Catch. Stretch & Catch has one goal - to help parents, caregivers and teachers teach all children how to read.

Amanda has used the Stretch & Catch method to teach reading to all ages and levels. Children who are gifted, children with learning disabilities and every level in-between have achieved success using Stretch & Catch. She has found that using Stretch & Catch's multi-sensory approach helps children understand how words work by pulling them apart and putting them back together. Stretch & Catch follows a developmentally appropriate spelling order that enables the parent, teacher, or caregiver to teach children Stretch & Catch words at their instructional level.

Amanda has her Bachelor's Degree in Elementary Education grades 1-8. She also earned her Master's Degree in Education as an Intervention Specialist with a certification in Moderate-Severe Special Education for grades K-12. In addition to teaching in elementary schools, Amanda spent three years as an instructor at Cleveland State University. There she taught undergraduates and graduates in the areas of Phonics Assessment, Phonics Instruction and Literature Based Reading.

In addition to being a full time mother, Amanda has also spent countless hours successfully tutoring children who have needed reading and spelling intervention.

She lives with her three children and husband in Cleveland, Ohio.

CPSIA information can be obtained
at www.ICGtesting.com
Printed in the USA
FFOW05n1302180815